The
MYSTERY
FANcier

Volume 5 Number 5
September/October 1981

The MYSTERY FANcier

Volume 5 Number 5
September/October, 1981

TABLE OF CONTENTS

The MYSTERY FANcier
(USPS:428-590)
is edited and published bi-monthly by Guy M. Townsend,
29 S. Church Street, West Chester, Pennsylvania 19380.
Contributions of all descriptions are welcomed.

SUBSCRIPTION RATES: Domestic second class mail, $12.00 per year (6 is-
sues); overseas surface mail, $12.00; overseas airmail, $15.00. Overseas subscribers please pay in international money order, check drawn
on U.S. bank, or currency; no checks drawn of foreign banks, please.

Second class postage paid at West Chester, Pennsylvania.

ISBN: 978-1-4344-3627-6

WILDSIDE PRESS

Mysteriously Speaking ...

In the five years since its inception, *The MYSTERY FANcier* has had eight different addresses. Never has one entire volume been mailed out from the same address. That has almost happened a couple of times before, but something always seems to come up at the last minute to keep it from being six issues in a row. The issue you now hold in your hand is the fifth to be mailed from the West Chester address, and the incurably optimistic among you may be thinking that the third time is the charm and that Townsend is finally going to stay in one place long enough to get through an entire volume of TMF without an address change. Well, forget it.

The peripatetic peregrinator is on the road again, and you should send your cards, letters, articles, reviews, charitable donations, and blackmail payments to me at this address:

1711 Clifty Dr.
Madison, IN 47250

It's a temporary address, for use only until we get settled down in Madison again. Madison is my wife's hometown, quite an attractive place in its own right, and it is there that the next chapter of the incomparable Townsend Saga is going to unfold. If I were giving these chapters titles, this one would be called either "How I Became the Publishing Mogul of the Mystery World," or "How I Went Bust Trying to Start a Publishing House Devoted to Analytical Works in the Mystery Field," depending on how it all turns out.

What the hell, I thought one day. I've written for newspapers, magazines, scholarly journals, and a few reference works; I've written s book with the help of some very capable collaborators; and I've edited a weekly newspaper and been associate editor of a national magazine. So why shouldn't I give publishing a try?

I know, I know. There are lots of reasons why I shouldn't, but the important thing is to think positive(ly), so let's not dwell on them, okay? Obviously, I couldn't compete with the big companies, publishing novels and such, but I figured there must be some area of publishing in which the little guy has a chance. And of course there is. Analytical works in the mystery genre are rarely best sellers (if you will pardon a little understatement), which is why most large publishing houses generally steer clear of them--short runs don't offer them enough profit to justify the effort. It occurred to me that if I were to do all the work myself--except, of course, for the actual

1

printing and binding--it was just barely possible that I could produce quality books at reasonable prices. The only customers, of course, would be libraries and dyed-in-the-wool mystery fans, but with a little luck there might be enough of them to keep the ship afloat. At any rate, there seemed to be at least a sporting chance that I could pull it off, so I decided to give it a try.

What I had, then, was this dream of starting a mystery publishing house, a large store of acquaintances upon whom I felt I could call for manuscripts (and for the evaluation of manuscripts submitted by others), and access to a limited amount of capital. Plus--and this is the most important element--a wife who was willing to let me work on this initially (and possibly permanently) unprofitable enterprise while she brought in a regular pay check.

Well, that was the start. Steve Stilwell (who does, after all, have some uses) suggested that a facsimile edition of volume one of *The Armchair Detective* would be the perfect book to launch the publishing operation, and Al Hubin, like Barkis, was willing. Al even wrote a special introduction for the facsimile edition. In the meantime, I had an ad drawn up for the next edition of TAD (I'll run a copy of it inside the back cover of this issue--bear in mind that it won't reproduce as well as the original), advertising the book for sale, and the publishing house took its first, halting steps. What am I calling it? Brownstone Books, of course. And if any of you have any ideas for books you'd like to do for Brownstone Books--analytical, biographical, bibliographical, or whatever--drop me a line. I'll be delighted to hear from you.

This thing has a plus side for TMF. Since I won't be punching a clock for someone else, I should have more time to devote to this magazine. As you are all painfully aware, I have always put TMF together on a dead run, with no time to spare for correcting typos, much less for editing the copy that fills its pages. Fortunately, TMF's contributors are a fairly literate bunch, and the quality of writing in these pages has always been passable and has usually been quite good indeed. Still, everyone can use an editor, and I look forward to being able to graduate to being TMF's editor in fact as well as in name-- right now, a more accurate title would be typist.

Dick Wenstrup has sent along a notice from *AB Bookman's Weekly* which should be of some interest to TMFers. A public auction is to be held in San Francisco November 18-20 of the 7,000 volume mystery collection of the late Adrian Goldstone. Adrian, some long-time TMFers will recall, was a subscriber to this magazine until his death a few years ago. A three-volume illustrated catalog will be available in October for $25 ($30 overseas) from California Book Auction Galleries, Inc., 385 Golden Gate Ave., San Francisco, CA 94102. Now here's a question--I thought Adrian had left his collection to some college; was that story false, or is the college unloading his collection? Anybody know?

THE SOLVING SIXTH

By Robert Sampson

Let us amuse ourselves with crime.
Stealing frightens; murder is tacky. Since actual crime
is tedious, let's devise a game.
In the 1920's, they played The Murder Game. Young ladies
who went all funny at a trapped mouse, blandly plotted the ex-
tinction of the Rich Old Man or the Crafty Lawyer. On a rainy
afternoon, any game is more acceptable than thinking, and you
can't decently play kissing games till dark.
If games jade, and the prospect of kissing is remote, perhaps a light discussion group. Each week, say, a member will
recount a crime of which he has personal knowledge. The others
will attempt to solve the crime and unmask the glowering criminal.
What fun!
What shall we call ourselves? We include Raymond West
(young writer), Joyce Lempriere (young artist), Sir Henry
Clithering (ex-Scotland Yard Commissioner), Dr. Pender (clergy-
man), and Mr. Petherick (lawyer).
That's five. Hardly enough. Miss Marple, will you join
us? You need only sit and listen. I'm sure it will be educa-
tional. (Miss Marple, elderly spinster, blushes faintly, lifts
one hand from her knitting in a depreciating gesture, and
acquiesces.)
Fine, fine, fine. We are six. We shall call ourselves The
Solving Six. How fine. Tuesday night, then. And each Tuesday
night thereafter.

That is the premise of "The Solving Six," a short story
series by Agatha Christie which began in Street & Smith's *Detective Story Magazine* in the issue dated June 2, 1928. The
series continued weekly into July, six stories in all. Later
appearances in *Detective Story* have not been traced, although
it is suspected that seven more appeared during 1929-1930.
After massive title changes, the stories were collected as *The
Tuesday Club Murders* (1932), the English title being *The Thir-
teen Problems*.
To say the worst immediately, let's agree that the series'
premise is artificial. It's one of those situational-idea
things that the 1920's relished so much and which later incited
such commentators as Raymond Chandler to flights of lyrical
venom. Then too, although each story is partially narrated by
a different person, most of them sound very much like Agatha
Christie, being articulate, sensitive, and cleverly obscure.
And finally, all the participants--defying nature's probabil-
ities--have personal knowledge of murder; the sheer volume of
crime encountered will surprise those Americans who consider
England a bastion of placidity.
These trivial quibbles aside, the series is splendid. It
represents the problem mystery in full flower, the puzzle, the
twist, the dazzling ending being of prime importance. Christie's
inventive mind flickers brightly above the limitations of the
form.
There is a reason for these stories to be narrated, rather
than unfolding as experiences. The whole purpose is to dis-

play Miss Marple in action. Aunt Jane Marple is at this time about sixty-five or seventy and seems everybody's grandmother. But even brilliant grandmothers ragely go rushing across the countryside sniffing out crime. Realistically, they sit knitting, listening, understanding.

Aunt Jane Marple is the classic armchair detective. Compared to her, Dupin is stagy and the Old Man in the Corner merely quaint. Miss Marple rarely has to seek out clues. By a fortunate stroke, each person narrating a story will mention precisely the correct clue to unravel the whole thing.

Miss Marple needs only that single clue. She is inhumanly quick. Her mind is utterly clear, utterly rational. No illusion dims its luster. Untroubled by bias or ramanticism, she embodies Victorian discipline without Victorian evasions.

Her field is people--their motives, and the things they do. For years she has studied the people of St. Mary Mead, the tiny village in which she lives.

For if you spend "a lifetime in a small village, and observe people carefully--you will know the essence of human behavior and motivations the world over. Details and scales of expression differ, and this is what confuses most people."[1]

So intensely has Miss Marple observed village life that nothing will surprise her, not evil, not even good. "There was no unkindness in Miss Marple," Christie remarks, "she just did not trust people." Observed experience is the basis for her detective work. She reasons by analogy: similar circumstances breed similar results.

There was a husband who murdered his wife in a very tricky way, by poison. And why? He was a sexually indulgent fellow with a pretty young girl servant in the house. That basic situation Miss Marple understands instantly. The tactical detail of how the poisoning was accomplished takes only a fraction longer.

That story is the first of the series. It is titled "The Solving Six" in the June 2, 1928 issue of *Detective Story Magazine*, being retitled "The Tuesday Night Club" for the book.[2] The problem posed is fumbled at artlessly by the other five club members. They are sophisticated people of the world, having seen Paris, London, and perhaps Beale Street. But they have not observed people--not the way this nice old lady from St. Mary Meade has observed them.

That is the silent joke of the series. This tall, thin old lady with faded blue eyes, his unworldly spinster with her hair piled up in white masses, is the real sophisticate of the group, the only one who understands the human heart.

She is "full of curiosity, knowing everything, hearing everything: the complete detective service in the home."[3] She wears an old-fashioned black dress, favors quantities of lace. Her fingers dart nimbly through the knitting as she listens.

So old-fashioned and, you know, like out of it.

She is old-fashioned enough to say a prayer when baffled.

---

[1] Robert A. Lowndes, "The Editor's Page," *Startling Mystery Stories #16*, Summer 1970, pp. 5-6.

[2] I have no information about the English magazine publication of these stories. My best guess in 1928. That Miss Marple first appeared in *Detective Story Magazine* a full-fledged pulp magazine heroine, is possible, although not very probable.

[3] Agatha Christie, *An Autobiography*, Dodd, Mead & Company, 1977, pp. 420-421.

She has no high opinion of doctors, finding the best medication in a cup of tansy tea. Nor is she convinced that the world's excellence has been increased with more powerful automobiles and hotter jazz.

She sits there quietly, a picture of gentle, ineffectual harmlessness, her fingers flickering among the wool strands. But all the while that level mind--sensitive, entirely aware, and fearfully dispassionate--listens, reasons from observed similarities, and finds the truth unchanging.

The Solving Six tag was hooked to several more story titles before disappearing--"The Solving Six and the Evil Hour" (June 9, later retitled "The Idol House of Astarte") and "The Solving Six and the Golden Grave" (June 16, retitled "Ingots of Gold"). The magazine titles show a deficiency of imagination that is most certainly not Mrs. Christie's.

The equally unfortunate title, "Drip, Drip" (Juen 23, elsewhere titled "The Blood-Stained Pavement") is attached to a splendid story. Miss Marple is in rare form. The mystery she penetrates at once, the instant she hears that a woamn in vivid clothing returned alone from a walk. Miss Marple remarks, "I don't think it is a fair problem to put to a man. I mean, we, being women, appreciate the point of the clothes."

The point of the problem (she says) is serial murder by a bigamous husband killing for insurance. She leaves the others quite flabbergasted. Dear old ladies are not supposed to know about serial murder for profit. "Mrs. Green," she says, "buried five children--and every one of them insured. I always find one thing very like another in this world."

Later she remarks to her nephew, Raymond West (whose worldly views of life have washed gloomily through several books): "I hope you dear young people will never realize how very wicked the world is."

"Where's the Catch" (June 30, retitled to "Motive vs. Opportunity") concerns a will which vanishes from a sealed envelope in a lawyer's safe. Only a blank sheet of paper is found. And how are we to explain this? Miss Marple does, drawing on recollections of youth. For the record, the lawyer, being a character of fiction, is entirely innocent.

"The Thumb Mark of Saint Peter" (July 7, title not changed for book publication) is Miss Marple's own story. The wife may, after all, have murdered the husband by feeding him poison mushrooms. He died rigid, muttering weirdly about a heap of fish--a pile of carp. Miss Marple must resort to a drug index before she understands, which is more than any of the other Solvers do.

By this story, the limitations of the Solving Six format were being discreetly ignored. New characters moved in. The sessions became ever less formal. The format of a narrated story remained--that and the unchangeable fact that Jame Marple, alone of the group, saw to the heart of each problem before anybody else could turn it around in his mind.

Finally the initial series melted into a drizzle of other Christie short fiction, including "Double Sin" (March 30, 1929, featuring Hercule Poirot).

But the first six stories were enough. Jane Marple, brightly launched, moved to fame, looking reality squarely in the face, buying baby presents, earning the reputation of being the greatest natural detective in England. Her cases appear in five short story collections (not all featuring her exclusively) and twelve novels. The final novel, *Sleeping Death* (1976), was also the last new Christie published. In this book, Aunt Jane is extremely old and physically feeble. But her mind still sheds its steady silver light, incredibly clear and undiminished.

WOLFE A HOWLER!

By Bob Napier

Like the rest of you, I greeted the news that Nero Wolfe would be a network television show with mixed emotions. Of course, I was pleased that the unique and wonderful character would get national attention, but I also feared that in the hands of the spineless pea-brains that produce current prime time fare Nero Wolfe would become a coast-to-coast embarrassment to all mystery fans. Luckily, not enough people tuned in to the show to give us an obvious black eye, but I imagine a common angst was felt among the mystery community before the season was half over, and by the last weekly humiliation a few of us were ready to deny we'd ever heard of Rex Stout, Nero Wolfe, or West Thirty-fifth Street.

What went wrong with the program is easy for any Wolfe fan to enumerate, but why it went wrong requires speculation--unless an insider happens to spill his guts. Still, you can't have been raised on television as I had been and not see what boob tube bigwigs consider mandatory elements in any TV drama-- action, sex, and the avoidance of anything that smacks of in- tellectualism. How Nero Wolfe even reached the pilot project stage must indeed reflect a sales pitch and a presentation that rates a spot in the Hustlers Hall of Fame, right next to the "Nixon's The One!" bumper sticker.

I'm not an unreasonable man, however. I realize that cer- tain alterations would be necessary before Wolfe could make the leap--or waddle--from the printed page to the home screen, and, in fact, I thought some changes would be prudent. For example, using the orchid rooms at a bare minimum, since it was Wolfe's inviolable sanctum. And little happened there that was germain to the plots, in most cases.

Naturally, the producers took the opposite tack and not only overused the orchid rooms but used them in such a way as to make the casual viewer believe that Wolfe consistently held court there.

Just for the heck of it I'd like to run down the list of regulars on the show and give my impression of them. After which I'll do my impre-sions of Walter Brennan, Henry Fonda, and Ed Sullivan.

William Conrad as Wolfe is just plain unfortunate. Conrad is a capable actor, although by no means brilliant, but he lacks the weight as a person and the range as an actor to carry the part effectively. His presence isn't commanding, and his voice lacks authority. His opulent surroundings dwarf him. He paces when he interrogates clients and suspects and giggles in glee when he conceives of a strategem. His idiosyncrasies have been changed for no good reason. It took him about eight shows to tell a man to sit because he "likes eyes at a level," but when the man refuses Wolfe replies, "Very well." Only to bel- low moments later because the man is standing. When, in the third or fourth show, Wolfe begins his lip routine, a woman tries to speak and is shushed by Archie, who explains that Mr. Wolfe is using his great genius and hates to be disturbed. In fact, when Wolfe goes into his lip routine he's so far lost in thought that no outside noises can reach him. Why they chose to alter Wolfe's personality in that way is as puzzling as the

time Archie told a woman that Wolfe is a blue-nosed Puritan,
which he isn't. He simply doesn't trust women or find them
very good company.

The list of non-Wolfean things that Conrad did as Wolfe
would make quite a list, and I have no intention of mentioning
them all, but it's enough to make one wonder why they bothered
paying the Stout estate for the rights to a character that they
had no serious thoughts of using in any but the most superficial
way. I'm also wondering why these alterations in the characters
were allowed in the first place, since some of them don't really
make much difference vis a vis the plot. Did Conrad do his
homework, or did he just scan one or two books and work from a
character sheet assembled by a TV hack writer and a producer
who wouldn't know a good idea if it bit him on the ass? And
if Conrad did do his homework and had a true picture of Wolfe
and his habits, why did he allow himself to play the role as he
did? I suspect he knew from the outset that the show was doomed
to eight episodes and he didn't think it worthwhile to make
waves. "You want me to cartwheel into the office and do a
mazurka on the globe? Great! Maybe it'll get me a guest shot
on Laverne and Shirley."

What disturbs me most about the bastardization of the character of Wolfe and the others is that it seems to underscore
the idea held by network brass that no TV drama can be made
without a lot of movement, noise, and color. Rather than present a story that is aimed at the mind--at least the part of
the mind that thinks--we're spoon fed images without substance
that are carefully pared down to fulfill the requirements of
our 28-second attention spans. I believe that's why soaps are
so successful. They titilate, tease, and then jump over to another scene. Like a juggler, they keep the objects moving, and
one is always in the air. Trying to force the mystery into
that format is a disaster, aesthetically if not financially.
No one minded that Charlie's Angles was pure pap, because the
obvious and highly exploited charms of the three girls, coupled
with the unchallenging plots, appealed to a sufficient number
of your friends, neighbors, and Neilsen families to make everyone connected to the show rich and famous--with the possible
exceptions of Robert Wagner and Natalie Wood. But, as the old
cop-out goes, I digress.

Archie Goodwin, as played by Lee Horsley, did a pretty fair
job of it I thought. It's a difficult role for many people to
accept because Archie is closer to a state of mind thana minute-
ly delineated character. We all have our own idea of an ideal
Archie, and what will satisfy one fan will horrify another.
Horsley has been called too handsome, a male-model type, and
he's too tall in relation to Wolfe (but Conrad's too short),
but I think in the most important area he did justice to the
part. That area is his understanding of the character and
Archie's job as Wolfe's right arm and occasional drover. I
liked Horsley's portrayal because it emphasized Archie's gentle
and persuasive manner and his sense of humor. Naturally he
suffered at the hands of the scriptwriters, along with everyone
else in the series. When he fears a bomb is in his car in one
show he doesn't bother trying to have it defused, but instead
uses a length of wire he carries around to engage the ignition
and blow the car to smitereens (that's Brooklyn for smither-
eens). Think about it. Why destroy a ten thousand dollar car,
camage adjacent cars, create a public hazard, and arouse the

unwanted attention of the police rather than open the hood and
see if a bomb is in the engine compartment. Nearly all car
bombs work either off the starter (electrically detonated) or
the manifold (heat detonated). If it were the latter type, his
trick would not have worked as it takes a couple of minutes for
the engine to reach the required temperature to activate the
detonator. It's obvious this little scene was thrown in because somewhere in that vast netherworld where TV execs slurp
martinis, back-slap, and dream of standing naked before a jeer-
ing crowd there lives an idea, almost a commandment in stone,
that all TV crime dramas must have at least one automobile de-
stroyed. A strange dictum when you consider the national love
affair we have as a people for our cars.

Be that as it may, it indicates that, however well Horsley
may have interpreted Goodwin's presence and manner, there was
no way he could control Goodwin's dialogue or scenes. I think
the producers lost an excellent bet in this series when they
ignored one of the key elements of the books which advanced the
story line and established a perfect point of view for the
reader/viewer--ergo, they should have had Archie narrate between
scenes. They could have fleshed out the plots, created the
Wolfe of the books, added to the whodunit element, and just
made the entire show more interesting. Look how snappy and
rich the Dragnet shows were. Jack Webb never filmed a shor of
a car rolling into a parking place or cruising down the street
without using the time to voice-over a bit of italic script.
It keeps the story moving and allows for better plotting.
Granted, the Nero Wolfe TV show wasn't as sloppy as many shows
are in that respect, but it could have been tighter and made
more interesting. So, while I liked the Archie they chose for
this show, I think he wasn't used to his full potential, and
he certainly was not accurately represented with regard to his
ability or intelligence. Again, I fault the producers, who
control this type of thing.

George Voskovec was a good Fritz but for some odd reason
was demoted from his major domo position to a kind of male Mrs.
Hudson. I suppose this was because Robert Coote, as Theodore
Horstmann, the orchid nurse, brought "audience identification"
with him, having been in The Rogues in 1964-1965, plus having
made many TV guest appearances, scores of movies and plays,
and--the cornerstone of his career--having been on Who's
There, a quiz/audience participation show broadcast during the
summer of 1952. They're probably still buzzing about that in
Bill Cullen's dressing room. It is these impressive credits,
probably coupled with the fact that he works cheap, that landed
Coote the Horstmann role, despite the fact that Horstmann sounds
Dutch or German. I don't remember Horstmann having much, if
anything, to say in the books, but in the show he's not only
garralous but a smartass and insubordinate to Wolfe. All this,
it seems, at the expense of Fritz's part. Bad casting and bad
thinking.

But bad casting really rears its head when Allan Miller
trots in as a poor excuse for Lt. Cramer. Cramer, the big,
gruff, read-eared, cigar-chewing cop, is suddenly a skinny,
needle-nosed wimp who flounces out of his chair like a prissy
chorus boy with wet nail polish. Pfui! My mother accurately
characterized him as a typical shoe salesman, and I agree--and
that may be giving him the best of it. Is this a sample of why
TV Guide's critic Robert Maclenzie calls it a "series that

faithfully translates the novels"? Or is he talking about
George Wyner as Saul Panzer? Saul, who's supposed to be a
little guy with a textbook poker face comes across as a large
oaf who affects a host of Nervous-Nellie habits for reasons
I've yet to fathom. He's not Saul; throw the bum out.
   No Orrie, no Fred, no Lon. Thank God and NBC for small
favors. I heard talk of a Purley Stebbins being there, but I
must have blinked and missed it. I will give them credid for
their Johnny Keems, but he was such a quick walk-on and bump-
off that it hardly balances the scales in NBC's favor.
   Mind you, with all these drawbacks I still liked the show
for the first half of the run. I expected TV to aberrate many
of the conventions of the novels, so when I saw something that
was right--Wolfe's yellow shirts and pyjamas, the attractive
brownstone, the beer ritual, the elevator, the lip routine--I
tended to give it greater weight than I gave the errors. Unfortunately, as the series progressed the number of correct
things seemed to fade and the number of wrong things began to
make quantum leaps. It reached a crescendo when Wolfe went all
gushy and moonstruck as he listened to the recorded yowlings of
his long lost love. I don't doubt that the loud "Bullshit!" I
yelled echoed from Cupertino to Bexley to West Chester, Pennsylvania.
   After that I sort of gave up hope, and my wall of tolerance
crumbled, allowing the realities of the show to flood in like
claims against the Howard Hughes estate. I missed the next
show because it was just too much trouble for me to get out of
bed at that ungodly hour, and when it faded away finally after
the last show I breathed a sigh of relief. If Rex Stout were
alive today he'd turn over in his grave.
   What really saddened me was the news that Orson Welles
would have been willing to play the part if NBC would have made
just a couple or three specials a year. I read that to mean TV
movies. To think that the perfect actor was willing to essay
the Wolfe role in a format condusive to a good plot that also
leaves room for character development.... If they could add to
that a producer willing and able to maintain the integrity of
the novels we could have had a classic on our hands.
   But nooooooo!
   They insisted on a series, and even as they made it there
was no doubt in anyone's mind that it would fail. It was made
to fail; it was scheduled against a show that would add to its
speedy ratings plunge and it was ultimately so misshapen that
even hard-core Wolfe fans wouldn't mourn its passing.
   Leave it to television, those million-dollar cretins, to
screw up something good that falls into their laps practically
ready-made. And I guess the viewing public has to share the
blame for the big travesty the moguls made of Wolfe. Let's
face it, is the mind that revels in Sheriff Lobo ready for a
Nero Wolfe?

ON FANS AND BOUCHERCONS

BY GUY M. TOWNSEND

Bouchercon is just around the corner, and you will find details
regarding it on the back cover. Many TMFer's have attended
Bouchercons in the past, but a great many others have not. In
hopes of nudging some of the latter group into giving it a try
this year, I am reprinting in this place a short piece I wrote
last year while I was playing newspaper reporter. Not a soul
ever commented on it, which says something about the people who
read that newspaper. Of course, it could also say something
about the way I write, though that's a thought I don't like to
entertain.

Once every year, over the Columbus Day weekend, mystery
fans from all over the country, as well as a few from abroad,
gather for the ostensible purpose of listening to speeches and
panel discussions arranged for their edification.

The location varies from year to year, rotating from the
east coast, to the mid-west, to the west coast, to the east
coast, etc. This year it was in Washington, D.C.

It is conceivable that some actually make the trip for the
purpose of attending the scheduled events, but most come primarily for the purpose of seeing and talking with each other.

The pre-arranged activities of Bouchercon--as the Annual
Anthony Boucher Memorial Mystery Convention is familiarly
called--merely provide an excuse for the get-together.

Bouchercons, it should be pointed out, are not professional conventions like those held every year by the American Bar
Association, or the American Historical Association, or any of
the countless other professional organizations.

The people who come to Bouchercons are not members of the
same professional association or organization. Some do belong
to the Mystery Writers of America, but it is not their common
membership in anything which draws them together. It is,
rather, their shared love for the mystery genre--and for each
other.

There are a number (albeit a small number when compared
with science fiction) of mystery fan magazines, regrettably
known as "fanzines," to which most of the people who attend
Bouchercons subscribe.

These fanzines are generally edited and published by one
individual, who receives the articles, reviews, and letters of
which his magazine consists from the fans who are his subscribers. The whole thing operates on a casual, friendly
level, although disagreements do from time to time arise.

Mysteries--using the word in its broadest sense--are the
most widely read books in the world, but not all people who
read mysteries can be called mystery fans.

A mystery fan--bear in mind that the word fan has the same
root as the word fanatic--does not merely read mysteries. He
likes--at the very minimum--not just to read the stories themselves, but to read *about* them and about the people who produce
them.

A mere mystery reader who likes Agatha Christie's stories
may eventually read every mystery Dame Agatha ever wrote, but

11

the mystery fan won't stop there; he will go on to read everything that has ever been written about Christie, about Hercule
Poirot, about Miss Jane Marple, and about any and all of the
many, many other characters Agatha Christie created.

Then the fan will go on to read everything he can lay his
hands on about radio and movie adaptations of Christie's works.
The most fanatical of Christie fans may collect tapes of the
radio adaptations and prints of the movies.

The difference between the common, garden variety mystery
reader and the mystery fan is that, while the fan loves everything about mysteries, the reader merely loves reading the
stories.

The fan's interest goes beyond the plots and characters in
the books--it encompasses everything that goes into the crea-
tion of the books and their plots and characters. The fan
wants to know everything there is to be known about the genre.

The reader may merely be interested in knowing whether or
not Raymond Chandler's first novel, *The Big Sleep*, is a good
read, but the fan also finds it interesting to know that Chandler wrote his first book when he was about fifty years old,
that *The Big Sleep* is made up of several reworked short stories
which originally appeared in the pulp magazine *Black Mask*, and
that Chandler, who was educated in an English public schook,
regarded himself (and wanted others to likewise regard him) as
a novelist and not just a mystery writer.

For the reader of mysteries these facts are extraneous to
the enjoyment of the novel; for the fan, they heighten its enjoyment immeasurably.

The people who attend Bouchercons are not mystery readers,
they are fans, and they love to share their enthusiasms.

They correspond via the mails and the telephone and through
the pages of the mystery fanzines, and once a year they gather
--as many of them as can afford the time and the money to do
so--and share their enthusiasms for a few days.

A curious thing happens at these gatherings. While the
subject of mysteries is never long out of the conversation,
talk focusses more on the people who write and read them than
on the mysteries themselves.

Stories about this or that writer--or this or that fan, for
that matter--are more likely to be heard than discussions of
plots or even characters in mystery stories.

It is as though mysteries were the fan's profession, and
when he gets together with his fellow professionals the shop-
talk is interlarded with friendly, personal, non-professional
topics as well.

That's the way it was at this year's Bouchercon. Washington in the fall is one of the world's loveliest cities, I am
told. I wouldn't know from personal experience, though, because I spent the entire weekend--except for taxi drives to and
from the airport--in the company of a few hundred friends and
fans, all of us so wrapped up with talking with and about each
other that what was happening outside of the hotel rooms and
the National Press Club, between which we scurried like indus-
trious ants, was of no consequence whatever.

After it was over I hopped into a cab at the hotel door and
said, "National Airport, please." The cabbie drove to the
corner and turned right.

Still remembering with pleasure the companionable hours I
just spent, I cast a disinterested eye out the window and ob-

served, "Pretty lawn," as we pulled away from the light. "That's the White House," the cabbie replied.

I had been in Washington from Friday to Sunday, within a block or two of the White House the whole time, and I hadn't even made an effort to look at it. It's a matter of getting your priorities straight.

"Oh," I said to the driver, and then went back to thinking of more important things, like the Bouchercon just past, and the one to come, in Milwaukee, next year.

NEWS NOTE

Professor Euell Parrish, Thorndyke Professor of Literary Ballistics at West Dakota State Teachers College and editor of *The Journal of Ratiocinative Research,* has announced the forthcoming publication of an anthology of historic lost works of detective fiction. Though a firm publication date has not been announced, Professor Parrish released the following list of probable contents, pending clearance of permissions with the authors' heirs:

The Enigma of the Surgeon's Collaborator
By Robert Eustace and Clifford Halifax
(This is the only joint work by the two famed consultants. More tales were planned, but they had a falling out over whose name would come first.)

"The Little Murder Case"
By S.S. Van Dine
(Involving the murder of a circus midget, this is the only Philo Vance short story. It gives the lie to the long-standing assumption that Van Dine was the only American of the Golden Age never to use a circus background.)

The Adventure of the Walking Hipflask
By Edmund Wilson
(The famed critic's only extant detective story, written some time in the twenties, reflects the dual influence of Doyle and Fitzgerald. Did its rejection shape Wilson's sour view of mystery fiction?)

Professor Parrish invites readers of *The MYSTERY FANcier* to submit other candidates for this anthology.

(Supplied by Jon Breen)

14

SPY SERIES CHARACTERS IN HARDBACK, IX

BY BARRY VAN TILBURG

DOSSIER #49: Sam Durell.
CREATED BY: Edward S. Aarons.
OCCUPATION: Agent for the CIA.
ASSOCIATES: General McFee, his boss; Deirdre Padgett, his girl-
friend.
WEAPONS: Smith & Wesson .38.
OTHER COMMENTS: Durell is a very violent agent who hates modern
gadgets. He is in a constant state of worry about his sur-
vival factor. The series started in the early fifties in
paperback. Books listed are not in the original order but
in the order they were published in in Britain.
Assignment--Suicide (Herbert Jenkins, 1964).
Assignment--Stella Marni (Herbert Jenkins, 1965).
Assignment--Carlotta Cortez (Herbert Jenkins, 1965).
Assignment--Mara Tirana (Herbert Jenkins, 1966).
Assignment--Treason (Herbert Jenkins, 1966).
Assignment--Zoraya (Herbert Jenkins, 1967).
Assignment--Burma Girl (Herbert Jenkins, 1967).
Assignment--Manchurian Doll (Herbert Jenkins, 1968).
Assignment--Black Viking (Gold Lion, 1971).
Assignment--Helene (Gold Lion, 1972).
Assignment--Maltese Maiden (Gold Lion, 1973).

DOSSIER #50: Lawrie Fenton.
CREATED BY: Michael Annesley.
OCCUPATION: Starts the series as an agent of the Foreign Office
and later takes over as head when Sir George Fawley dies.
ASSOCIATES: Sir George Fawley, his boss; Stella, his first wife;
Alex, his second wife; Stephen Brooks, his friend and fel-
low agent.
WEAPONS: Prefers a knife but can also use a gun.
OTHER COMMENTS: Fenton is a tall, dark, thin fellow who loves
disguises. He can be a society person or a down-on-his-
luck criminal with equal ease. Unlike Durell or Carter,
Fenton differs in appearance and in ideas with age.
Room 14 (Harrap, 1935; published as *Fenton of the Foreign Office*
by Robert Speller, 1937).
Spies in the Web (Harrap, 1936).
Spies in Action (Harrap, 1937).
The Missing Agent (Harrap, 1938).
The Vanished Vice-Consul (Harrap, 1939).
Unknown Agent (Harrap, 1940).
Spy Against the Reich (Harrap, 1940).
Suicide Spies (Harrap, 1944).
An Agent Intervenes (Harrap, 1944).
Spy--Counter Spy (Stanley Paul, 1945).
They Won't Lie Down (Stanley Paul, 1946).
Spies Abounding (Stanley Paul, 1947).
Spy Corner (Stanley Paul, 1948).
Spy Island (Stanley Paul, 1948).
Lights that Did not Fail (Stanley Paul, 1949).

DOSSIER #51: Ed Noon.
CREATED BY: Michael Avallone.
OCCUPATION: Noon starts the series as a hardboiled private in-
    vestigator; he later becomes a spy for the President.
ASSOCIATES: The President, his boss; Captain Mike Monks, a
    homicide detective for the N.Y.P.D. (and his friend);
    Melissa Mercer, his secretary and girlfriend.
WEAPONS: Noon became used to the .45 Colt automatic in the Army
    in Korea and has kept to it ever since.
OTHER COMMENTS: Noon is a tough, cynical type of person, which
    makes him excellently equipped for the espionage business.
    His hobbies are women, baseball, and old movies. Books
    dealing with espionage are marked with an asterisk.
The Tall Dolores (Holt, Rinehart, 1953; Barker, 1956).
The Spitting Image (Holt, Rinehart, 1953; Barker, 1957).
Dead Game (Holt, Rinehart, 1954; W.H. Allen, 1959).
Violence in Velvet (W.H. Allen, 1958).
The Case of the Bouncing Betty (W.H. Allen, 1959).
The Case of the Violent Virgin (W.H. Allen, 1960).
Meanwhile Back at the Morgue (Muller, 1961).
The Alarming Clock (W.H. Allen, 1961).*
The Bedroom Bolero (Brown Watson, 1964; published as *The Bolero
    Murders* by Hale, 1972).
The Living Bomb (W.H. Allen, 1963).
The Brutal Kook (W.H. Allen, 1965; Brown Watson, 1966).
The Fat Death (W.H. Allen, 1966).
The February Doll Murders (W.H. Allen, 1966).*
The Horrible Man (Robert Hale, 1968).*
The Flower-Covered Corpse (Robert Hale, 1969).
Killer's Highway (Robert Hale, 1970).*
Death Dives Deep (Robert Hale, 1971).*
The Ultimate Client (Robert Hale, 1971).*
The Moving Graveyard (Hale, 1973).*
The Girl in the Cockpit (Robert Hale, 1974).
Ed Noon in London (Robert Hale, 1974).*
Kill Her--You'll Like It (Robert Hale, 1974).
The Big Stiffs (Robert Hale, 1977).*
Dark on Monday (Robert Hale, 1978).

It's About Crime

By Marvin Lachman

NOTES ON RECENT READING

The best-seller list is dotted with mystery-related exam-
ples of what I would call the "cop-out" school of literature.
Stephen King's *Firestarter* is about a little girl who can ig-
nite objects merely by looking at them. John Gardner has made
the list by resurrecting James Bond. Len Deighton's *XPD* is
about the search for proof that Churchill once did business
with Hitler. Other recent fiction has been based on the in-
discretions (or worse) of Presidents from George Washington to
Richard Nixon. Ross Thomas's *The Morida Man* (1981) is about a
U.S. President, his brother, and the ruler of Lybia. William
F. Buckley takes cheap shots at Truman and Ike and pads his
books with imaginary conversations between Dean Acheson and
Allen Dulles.

I call these books "cop-outs" because there is no attempt
to come up with really well-thought out plots. Instead, the
story is built upon the wildest, flimsiest, and catchiest gim-
mickry. Elsewhere, I have written about the hostage-hijacking
school of literature, exemplified by Alistair MacLean having
the President of the United States kidnapped in the middle of
the Golden Gate Bridge.

If I decry implausibility, why am I not a fan of Rex Burns
after reading his first two books, the Edgar-winning *The Al-
varez Journal* (1975) and *The Farnsworth Score* (1977). If they
are anything, they are realistic, dealing with the stuff of
modern crimes: drugs, police infiltration of dope rings, in-
formers, et al. The dialogue and the crimes are from the
streets, not someone's rose garden. That's just the problem;
there is no element of escape here. The reader gets the worst
of all possible worlds--the dreariness of cheap crimes without
the facts that make good books about true crime worthwhile.

Once again I had to go back to the Golden Age to keep my
interest. Francis Beeding's *Death Walks in Eastrepps* (1931)
comes well recommended. Vincent Starrett called it one of the
ten best mysteries of all time when it came out, and he repeat-
ed this as late as 1965 when he did an outrageously bad introduction for a hardcover reprint in Norton's ill-fated Seagull
Library of Mystery and Suspense. I guess I had better document
my charge about Starrett before Messrs. Nieminski and Stilwell
lynch me. Though he doesn't actually disclose the killer,

17

Starrett gives away almost every other surprise. This, mind you, is not in a critical work dissecting a classic but in the introduction to a new edition that readers are presumably ready to start.

Starrett even commits a careless error, claiming that Beeding's famous numbered series of Colonel Granby novels were published in order, e.g., *The One Sane Man, The Two Undertakers, The Three Fishers,* et al. Actually, the first book in the series was *The Six Proud Walkers* (1928). It was followed by *The Five Flamboys* (1929). *The One Sane Man* did not come along until 1934, by which time Beeding had already used five numbers in his titles.

Just because Vincent Starrett had an off day is no reason to miss *Death Walks in Eastrepps.* The edition to buy and read is the brand new paperback by Dover ($4.00). It has no introduction and needs none. The book speaks for itself, a throwback to a time when authors felt the need to provide mysteries that were long, inventive, and contained many surprises. A series of murders takes place in an East Norfolk resort town. The puzzle is a good one, though the identity of the killer is far from impossible to guess. Things move at a fast pace, and a bonus is the excellent description of the effect of these murders on a resort during its summer season.

Even better from Dover (at $3.50) is Cyril Hare's first mystery, *Tenant for Death* (1937). Hare generates the kind of intellectual excitement that used to be present in so many mysteries. The facts are presented to the reader and, if the puzzle is not as complex as Ellery Queen in his heyday, there is still much for the reader who wishes to compete with the detective.

Hare's sleuth is Inspector Mallett who, after appearing in Hare's first three books, began playing second fiddle to the author's later detective, Francis Pettigrew. Mallett is a detective we can respect and identify with. I can visualize a subdued Leo McKern (of Rumpole fame) playing him on the screen. There is humor in *Tenant for Death*, and it is reasonably subtle. Hare has a good ear for language and introduces (and demolishes) a few pompous individuals. There is not a great deal of description, and that is good because too much tends to slow a mystery down. There is just enough for the reader to supply his own imagination and set his own scenes.

MISCELLANEOUS MYSTERIOUS MISHMASH

Information about the mystery and mystery writers seems to turn up all over the place. Last year, there was the obituary of the famous British novelist, C.P. Snow, who started and finished his long, illustrious career with detective novels. On June 18, 1981, came the death at age sixty-nine of Pamela Hansford Johnson, who was Snow's widow and a well-known British novelist and playwright. With her first husband, the Australian historian-journalist Gordon Neil Stewart, she had written two mysteries--*Tidy Death* (1940) and *Murder's a Swine* (1943, U.S. title: *The Grinning Pig*)--under the joint pseudonym Nap Lombard.

Victoria Lincoln died on June 13, 1981, at age seventy-six. She was best known for a 1934 novel, *February Hill*, which be-

came a popular play and film as *Primrose Path*. However, before
becoming a mainstream novelist, Lincoln had written a mystery
novel, *The Swan Island Murders* (1930). Her most recent published book was *A Private Disgrace: Lizzie Borden by Daylight*
(1967).

The above writers are not the only ones to write mysteries
as well as other fiction/non-fiction. One of the most successful writers inside and outside our genre is Lady Antonia Fraser.
She has done two novels regarding TV reporter-detective Jemima
Shore, *Quiet as a Nun* (1977) and *The Wild Island* (1978), both
reprinted by Ace at $1.95 and $2.25 respectively. However, she
is more famous as a historian-biographer, having written such
well-regarded books as *Mary, Queen of Scots* and *Cromwell, Lord
Protector*. Dell, under its Delta imprint, has just published a
trade paperback version at $8.95 of her highly acclaimed *Royal
Charles*. What a great title for this summer! However, it is
about Charles II of seventeenth century fame. Good history is
much like good detective fiction as the author (detective) sifts
through available facts, trying to get at the truth.

I'm setting some time aside soon to read Fraser, both her
fiction and her non-fiction. While waiting to read her, I've
been reading *about* her. She has had a much publicized affair
with the British playwright, Harold Pinter. It began when Lady
Antonia left Sir Hugh Fraser, her husband of twenty-one years
and father of their six children. She lived with Pinter five
years before they recently married. During that time Pinter's
then-wife, actress Vivian Merchant, claimed her husband had
been "possessed" by Lady Antonia. Who needs *People* or other
similar magazines when Lachman is around with the really important gossip?

Muriel St. Clare Byrne is not exactly a household name.
She collaborated with Dorothy L. Sayers on a successful play
version of the latter's last novel, *Busman's Honeymoon*. She
was also the literary executor of Sayers' estate. Now, at the
age of eighty-six, she has edited her master work, *The Lisle
Letters*, a collection of over two thousand letters which will
tell the interested reader an incredible amount about life in
Tudor England. If you're intrigued, save your money. It is
being published by the University of Chicago Press, in six
volumes, at $250--until December 31. After that, the price
goes up.

During June I kept seeing and hearing references to Dashiell
Hammett on PBS-TV. First there was an interview with Lillian
Hellman about him. She described their thirty year affair as
"passionate," but somehow her tone of voice belied the word.
Pat Bond did a one-woman show as Gertrude Stein, who, when she
finally returned to the United States in 1934 after a thirty
year absence, expressed the desire to meet--you guessed it--
Hammett when she was in Hollywood. PBS also was showing the
excellent 1935 film version of Hammett's *The Glass Key* with
George Raft, Edward Arnold, and a very young Ray Milland.

Mystery * File

Short Reviews
By Steve Lewis

Henry Kitchell Webster. *Who Is the Next?* Perennial Library, 1981, 310 pp.; first published in 1931.

I hope you've all seen the books in this series of paperbacks from Perennial. They include such authors as Nicholas Blake, Matthew Head, Elspeth Huxley, Lange Lewis, and Anna Mary Wells--writers of the classical sort of mystery novel that you otherwise just don't see in print at all anymore.

My advice? Give them some support, and help keep Harper, the parent company, aware that there are still some mystery fans out here. (And I don't think you'll regret the money spent on something good to read, either.)

For a book first published fifty years ago, *Who Is the Next?* is amazingly fresh and up-to-date. The subdued, unacknowled love interest between a guardian and his much younger ward would not be played quite the same today, but unencumbered by today's slightly more "enlightened" attitudes, Webster's version of this scenario has an attraction that is both pleasing and frustrating--as it was meant to be then, and as it still is today.

Nor would Camilla Lindstrom's airplane be of the same model and vintage, but in the process of becoming a woman, there's no better symbol of her budding independence, even today. Her childhood is in the process of disaypearing, and as it does her guardian, Prentiss Murray, realizes that he is falling in love with her.

Well, of course it's more than a love story. (Need you ask?) Camilla's aged grandfather is murdered, and almost immediately afterward so is Miss Parsons, his newly acquired secretary and companion. Also soon on the scene is Camilla's prodigal brother, and of course there are numerous mysterious strangers seen lurking around the estate.

There is a good reliance on fate (on the part of the murderer), and some good detective work (on the part of the police). My only real complaint is that too much of the latter is done behind the scenes, and it comes out only in retrospect, at the end.

But for mystery, vintage atmosphere, and romance, with one of the spunkiest heroines you'd ever want to meet, this book would be hard to beat.

I read the last one hundred pages in twenty minutes.

That's three times my usual reading speed. (A)

Patrick McGinley. *Bogmail*. Tichnor & Fields, 1981, 259 pp.;
first published in England in 1978.

Billed as "a novel with murder," this sprightly philosoph-
ical tale of Ireland has several things going for it, few of
which have to do with what's usually involved in crime fiction.
The first and the most obvious of these is the rich, loamy
taste and feel of rural Ireland--the land of soggy peat bogs
and warm country taverns, those eternal warehouses of good-
natured camaraderie and unfailing intellectual pursuit (mostly
male).
When the keeper of one of these fine establishments permanently quenches one of the more obnoxious of his adopted daughter's suitors, an unknown observer spots him disposing of his
victim in a nearby bog. Hence the title.
And thus it is that the blackmailer is the mysterious Mr.
X involved, not the killer. The only clues provided are the
notes he sends nervously awaiting prey. The end of the story
brings at last the disclosure of his identity, but very nearly
only accidentally so. Only in some intangible, unsettled--and
unsettling--sense can it be said that justice has been done,
if at all.
This is McGinley's first work of fiction. In it he does a
fine job of blending character, atmosphere, and plot into something that's just a sideways step out of the ordinary in the
world of the detective novel. I'll be looking forward to his
next book. (B plus)* (*Reviews so marked have appeared earlier in the Hartford *Courant*.)

Anna Clarke. *Letters from the Past*. Doubleday/Crime Club,
1981, 181 pp., $9.95.

Anna Clarke writes fine, intelligent Victorian mystery fiction. Unfortunately, when she places the action in the present,
as she does here in her latest melodrama, the dialogue jars a
bit at first, since nobody has talked quite like this since the
1920's, at the latest.
Wuth the passing of one of his flock (and under mysterious
circumstances, it must be added), a vicar's indiscreet past has
come back to haunt him, as it always will. His torment, based
on a misguided lack of communication between his daughter and
himself, is hot and feverish, and blackmail is the least of his
worries.
The ending is weak, marred by sudden revelations and some
hitherto unsuspected major participants in the plot, but Miss
Clarke obviously knows how to keep a story moving. A little
more care was needed in working this one out, but perhaps all
she had to do with her little drama was to have set it in the
proper century. It might have done wonders. (B minus)*

Robert B. Gillespie. *The Crossword Mystery*. Raven House,
1980, 190 pp., $1.75.

As I understand it, the first four Raven House titles (this
is #3) were sent out as advance samples to at least some, if
not all, of the subscribers to Harlequin's line of romance
titles. I don't know if the story is true, but if it is, I

wonder what those women thought of this book. As the title indicates, it's purely a puzzle story, but the language used is
often surprisingly crude and foul--of the four-letter variety.
There's also one pretty good sex scene, and one fairly
brutal, which is not so good. This does not count the murder
of Mary Cross, Rocky Caputo's predecessor as the crossword
editor of the *New York Herald-Courier*. Means of death: starva-
tion in a locked room, complicated by cirrhosis of the liver.

The puzzle itself--a message in cryptograms, only later as
a crossword--is major league, but as we all know, cleverness
alone does not a novel make. Gillespie shows promise, but he
needs more seasoning. Overall, I'd say Triple A ball in the
minors, at best, and if you can't stand crossword puzzles at
all, you can probably skip this one. (C)

Dorothy Simpson. *The Night She Died.* Scribner's, 1981, 188
    pp., $9.95.

In the world of crime fiction, there seems to be an unwrit-
ten law that a new private eye has to have a gimmick, a little
quirk of behavior, perhaps, that will help him (or her) stand
out from all the others. There is a similar theory for policemen, and it holds that because of the nature of their job, they
need humanizing: a loving family, perhaps. Teething babies.
Bad backs.
Inspector Thanet is lucky. He has all three.
His current case involves a murdered woman. Who killed
her? Her husband, with whom she was seeing a marriage counsel-
or? Her thwarted, amorous boss? The determined ex-suitor?
Thanet's investigation also takes him back into the past,
over his sergeant's objections, to dig up an unsolved murder
the victim may have witnessed as a child. The problem is that
looking into this old case is as dry and uninteresting as pok-
ing around in a pile of dusty bones, and it'd be awfully easy
to give the story up as routine right here.
And this you shouldn't do, as Simpson has a terrific surprise in store for the persevering reader who sticks it out to
the end. I suspect there'll be a good many people who'll never
reach it. Exquisitely plotted, and ploddingly told--a sad combination. (D)*

Max Byrd. *California Thriller.* Bantam, 1981, 217 pp., $2.25.

As it happened, this book has been sitting on my shelf for
quite a while, tempting me to pick it up and read it every time
I looked at it. I finally did so, and now that I've done it,
I'm not so sure I'm glad I did. The anticipation was far better than anything reading it actually produced.
Mike Haller is a San Francisco private eye. He specializes
in missing persons. A newspaper writer has disappeared, and
Haller is hired to find him. The only clue he finds is a collection of pictures of mutilated cats, and a phone number.
Haller has his own personal code of ethics, of course, the
same as any self respecting PI, and a girl friend named Dinah,
who is a lady psychologist. Comparisons with Spenser and his
friend named Susan Silverman are inevitable, but they should be
avoided. Haller is but a pale imitation, whether it's intended

or not, and Max Byrd is no Robert B. Parker.
The story doesn't move. It has no life. It lies down,
rolls over, and plays dead. Pulp fiction may not ever have
been considered great literature, but by golly the plots pulled
the reader into the story. You didn't have to force yourself
to pick it up and read another couple of chapters, night after
night.
I don't think the scary mad scientist scene helped much
either, and it's the highlight of the book. (C)

Kelley Roos. *Murder on Martha's Vineyard*. Walker, 1981, 197
pp., $9.95.

Readers in this part of the country are likely to pick this
one up solely because of its title, read a page or two, and
then find themselves suddenly hooked and being reeled in by one
of the most suspenseful thrillers I've read in quite some time.
The background turns out to be only incidental. Audrey and
William Roos, the names behind the joint Kelley Roos by-line,
are a couple of old pros, however, who know all the tricks in
snagging the reader's attention and, more importantly, in hold-
ing it.
A young newly-wed returns to the island with her new husband, only to find resentment still blazing on the part of one
of the natives, who thinks she got off too easily when she was
acquitted for the murder of her first husband.
She hires an old, used-up private eye to help clear her
name, and he does a pretty good job of detective work before
he's finished, but too late. Situations where kidnapping is
involved always produce a tremendous amount of tension, and
here's no exception.
I don't want to give away too much, but while a good deal
of what follows is predictable enough, you shouldn't really expect a happy ending. Not completely, that is. (B plus)*

John Brett. *Who'd Hire Brett?* St. Martin's, 1981, 173 pp.,
$9.95.

Funny detective stories are few and far between, even
counting those not intended to be, but which are anyway. This
one, I'm convinced, was meant to be.
John Brett, who is both author and leading character, is
often simply hilarious, in a snooty, smart-alecky way most reminiscent of a modern-day Wodehouse, without, however, the use
of a plot quite as tightly knit. In his genial, dim-witted,
and amateurishly clumsy fashion, Brett proves that the answer
to the question of the title is, "No one. No one at all."
But for a friend, he'll do a favor. Here in this country
from his native England on a regular remittance of hush money,
he helps the Beverly Hills police solve this case of the statue
with the broken toe, and in so doing he also saves a lady friend
from a murder charge.
In the end Brett proves he's been sharper than he's let on,
as well. Nevertheless, while you'll find that the clues for
the reader to blissfully stumble over were really there, I'm
still sure that you'll find your greatest pleasure in this rol-
licking California comedy caper somewhere else altogether. (B)*

Raoul Whitfield. *The "Virgin" Kills*. Knopf, 1932, 270 pp.

If you've never read the book, right now you probably have
the same wrong-headed idea of what the title means as I did
when I picked it up, not long ago. The *Virgin* is a boat; a
yacht, to be precise. A murder is committed on board. The
victim is the owner, a gambler named Vennell.

And even before that another murder has taken place. The
leading oarsman of the California shell is somehow poisoned,
and he collapses just before the finish of the big Hudson River
collegiate regatta. That California loses as a direct result
has obviously a great deal to do with the plot.

Vennell had just as obviously been expecting trouble, however. Along with the many society guests he has on board, he
also has a newly-acquired bodyguard, a hard-boiled hoodlum by
the name of O'Rourke. As a not-always-successful interface between the slick set and the underworld from which he clearly
comes, Nick O'Rourke is the object of some amusement and con-
jecture. He is probably the best developed character in the
book.

The repartee is dated and, mired in subtleties no longer
operative, it no longer has the bite it might once have had.
The pace picks up considerably after the murders occur, and we
have a full-fledged detective novel on our hands. Even though
the story is complexly motivated, I might warn you that the
obvious person did it.

Note that that doesn't mean that you'll catch on at all,
any more than I did! (B)

Lawrence Kinsley. *The Red-Light Victim*. Tower, 1981, 319 pp.,
$2.50.

The title and the cover design (multiple shots of a half-
nude dancer) are a trifle misleading. Yes, I know that in the
world of paperback advertising that's hardly anything new, but
here the publishers (who I naively suppose had a final say in
the matter) had a glorious opportunity to cash in on the anti-
nuke fad that's sweeping the country, and what do they pick out
as the essential ingredient in this book instead? Sex, that's
what. Can you dig it?

Jason O'Neil is the hero, a Boston-based private eye who's
hired by his former girl friend's roommate to find her. She's
a physics major and a top student at B.U., and she's suddenly
disappeared. The trail leads O'neil to the Combat Zone all
right, but only briefly. (But long enough for the cover shots
to be taken, huh?)

Jennifer (that's her name) was also a high echelon member
of the campus anti-nuclear organization, which, mixed with a
little Cosa Nostra involvement, happens to be enough to fill
out the rest of the book, with a long ways to go. It seems the
group plans to ... but that's for you to read and find out,
isn't it?

As a mystery, the book rambles on for too long (note the
number of pages), but its tone, wholly pessimistic about the
age of the atom, is probably more effective in its purpose
than a truckload of slogan-spouting rock stars, movie actresses,
and other uninformed but self-proclaimed experts.

Nevertheless, and all social significance aside, the characters *are* vividly drawn, and the detective work is effective

enough to suggest that Jason O'Neil is worthy of an encore. You'll have to give him some time, though. He was pretty emotionally wrapped up in this one. (B minus)

Robert B. Parker. *A Savage Place*. Delacorte Press/Seymour Lawrence, 1981, 184 pp., $10.95.

Spenser, the introspectively macho private eye from Boston, heads for Hollywood in this, his latest adventure. He's been hired as a bodyguard by a female TV reporter hot on the trail of a burgeoning scandal in the movie industry, but Southern California does not really seem to be his style.

He seems to flounder more than usual, as much out of his element as Philip Marlowe, for example, would be in New England. Yet with it all, Spenser's personality and personal code of behavior are as strong as ever, and flashes of his irreverent self can't help but come shining through.

In *Early August*, which appeared earlier this year, the key to the story was adolescent growing pains; here it is female dependency, and the struggle of women to succeed in a man's world. Candy Sloan wants the story she is covering to be hers alone, but she finds she needs Spenser for protection. She also finds she needs more than "feminine wiles."

The male-female fireworks produced are by themselves more than worth the price of admission, but the twists of the plot-- and Spenser's slowness in following them up--are designed not with the detective part of the tale in mind, but often serve only to hang the framework of the other half of the story that Robert B. Parker has to tell.

The novel that results is choppy and uneven, but no true fan of Spenser would dare miss it. Nor would anyone else who wants to know what's going on in the forefront of the private eye novel today. (A minus)*

Elizabeth Daly. *Death and Letters*. Dell/Murder Ink, 1981, 175 pp., $2.25; first published in 1950.

It's nice to see some of Elizabeth Daly's work back in print again. Her books are increasingly hard to find in used paperback shops, and the demand for them is high, as Carol Brener, the proprietress of Murder Ink, most assuredly well knows.

And I've known it, too, for quite some time now, and yet I've never gotten around to reading anything by her until now. This book, done toward the end of Miss Daly's writing career, was my introduction to Henry Gamadge, and do you know, from reading it I'm still not sure what it is exactly that he does for a living. Private eye work, apparently, but dealing primarily with bookish matters, perhaps?

Which certainly doubles the appeal to mystery fans, most of whom are collectors and savers of one sort or another.

In this case, a message via a crossword puzzle, and a Gamadgian response, with a little help from G.K. Chesterton, help spring a lady whose family has shut her up in her room as mentally incompetent. It seems she suspects something wrong about her husband's "suicide." One of the family knows for a fact there was. The others are merely afraid of scandal.

At first Daly's storytelling methods seem rather dry and

aloof, more British in tone than American, but the effect begins to diminish as the characters and the procedings start to sort themselves out a bit. The quiet little climax/resolution only serves to reinforce the obvious statement. Here is the complete antithesis of the Mickey Spillane school of writing! (B plus)

Charlotte MacLeod. *The Palace Guard*. Doubleday/Crime Club, 1981, 183 pp., $9.95.

If you like mysteries made in Boston, here's one for you. (Strangely enough, not since radio's long-running *Johnny Dollar* series has there been much going on in Hartford. Janice Law's recent *Death Under Par* is an exception that comes first to mind.)
I've missed the first two books in this series, but apparently Sarah Kellings has lost her husband, a man much older than herself, and as a result she's been forced to take in boarders. They are a motly lot, taken from many different segments of Bostonian society--none very high.
One of them is an art expert named Max Bittersohn, who combines romancing his landlady with helping her solve the murders of two guards at one of Boston's lesser-known museums.
Keep your eye on the motive. Many digressions later, cleverly disguised as part of the murder investigation, it turns out to have been the missing essential ingredient. Charlotte MacLeod has a knack for inventive characters and an eye for the humor in a situation, and besides--it also keeps our eye off the shell that's had the pea tucked safely inside it all along. (B)

James M. Reasoner. *Texas Wind*. Manor, 1980, 201 pp., $1.95.

Rumor has it that Manor has gone bankrupt. I don't know if it's true or not, but the fact remains that I haven't seen any of their product in over a year, and distribution was pretty good around here before that.
And I have never seen this book anywhere for sale. If James Reasoner hadn't sent me a copy personally, I'd have never seen it period. All this leads me to the fairly safe conclusion that if you haven't obtained a copy for yourself by now, you probably won't.
It's a pity, too, because it just may be the best book Manor ever published. They evidently never knew what they hae either, because the back of the book is filled with ads for their *western* novels.
And this is a private eye book, for crying out loud. Cody's home town is Fort Worth, and I guess maybe he wears cowboy boots, but that's about it. He's hired to find a mi-sing daughter, who maybe has run off with her best friend's boy friend--or has she been kidnapped?
There are a few false notes here (one of which led me into thinking up a whole new ending), and I thought Cody's love affair with Janice, the new light of his life, came on too fast, but Reasoner has a deceptively smooth, easy-to-read style that helps you forget you've read hundreds of stories like this a hundred times over. Never really flashy in any sense of the word, but a solid job through and through.

Bill Pronzini. *Hoodwink*. St. Martin's, 1981, 216 pp., $10.95.

Collecting pulps is today a rather specialized--and expensive--hobby. These were the cheap-paper magazines with the colorfully lurid covers that simply inundated the country's reading habits throughout the second quarter of the century. Fiction for the most part, they have since been superseded in providing escape literature for the millions by the paperback novel and, of course, now by television.

A Convention of pulp collectors therefore makes for an extremely esoteric gackground for Pronzini's nameless private eye to solve not one, but two locked room mysteries. "Nameless," as he is known, collects pulps himself, and since they have always played such a central part in his life--even to his choice of career, even though this is the first time they have taken over one of his adventures so completely--who better should be at hand?

The plot also involves a thirty-year-old case of plagiarism, but it is the musty odor of these aging receptacles of America's yesterdays that permeates the story from beginning to end. "Nameless" is a soppy, sentimental slob still sharp enough to solve the murders, however, and to whom something else nice happens as well. (B plus)*

Verdicts
(More Reviews)

Joseph Wambaugh. *The Glitter Dome*. Morrow, 1981, 295 pp., $12.95.

When Joseph Wambaugh was a cop, his novels about the police tended to be sober, solemn, and, as titles like *The New Centurians* and *The Blue Knight* suggest, eminently respectful of the force's public image. When he resigned after fourteen years' service to become a full-time writer, he used his freedom to explore new ways of presenting the cop's-eye view of life. In *The Choirboys* (1975) Wambaugh borrowed from *Catch-22* to create a street world full of raunchiness, sick jokes, episodic structure, outrageously illegal police conduct, and subliminal religious symbolism. He returns to this vein in *The Glitter Dome* but superimposes a storyline straight out of the classical detective novels, with a mysterious murder, a circle of suspects, and even an Ellery Queen-like double solution.

The main characters are impotent lush Al Mackey and morbidly religious Marty Welborn, veteran L.A.P.D. homicide investigators who, like most Wambaugh cops, have been eaten alive by psychological wounds suffered in the line of duty. Their assignment is to "clear" (which doesn't necessarily mean to solve) the murder of a top Hollywood producer whose body was found in a bowling alley parking lot, and the tangled trail takes them through movie studios and roller discos and massage parlors and Beautiful People parties. Meanwhile, three other pairs of cops--two funny scruffy narcs, a couple of overweight neanderthals, and a team of sadistic "street monsters"--are out on cases which every so often happen to unearth a lead in the major murder. Mackey and Welborn have to cope with several cleverly lying suspects (including one with a storybook Perfect Alibi) before a combination of deduction and dumb luck enables them to both "clear" the case on the books and identify a Least Likely Person as the real killer. By then, of course, both the main investigation and the dozens of peripheral characters and events have given us multiple object lessons in the stresses that foul up policemen's lives.

The most rabid cop-hater in America couldn't create officers as superficially repulsive as Wambaugh's. They are drunks, dopers, womanizers, flagellators, suicidal, sadistic, foul-mouthed, and venal. Some live for nothing but to maim and kill on the street, and the best of them fake evidence, beat suspects, perjure themselves in court, and violate constitutional

28

rights on a daily basis. They can't communicate with outsid-
ers, and they talk to each other mainly in four-letter words
and racial insults. Small wonder that director Robert Ald-
rich's movie version of *The Choirboys* portrayed all the cops
as fascist beasts! But Wambaugh's point, subtly established
through pervasive religious imagery, is that the police are not
just heroes but the Christs of the city, taking upon themselves
the pain of seeing human nature at its most hideous, suffering
for the rest of us in order to save us. For him the officers
are blue-robed street priests set apart by a special mark. This
is a hard doctrine, but Wambaugh's best-drawn characters, like
the self-crucifying Marty Welborn, make it almost credible, at
least for the duration of the book.

There are flaws in *The Glitter Dome*--too much self-indul-
gent satire on Hollywood wheeling-and-deeling, loss of control
over the whodunit elements near the end--and the abundance of
stomach-turning incidents will offend the squeamish. But Wambaugh's unique combination of grotesque characters, garish
evenst, and gross humor still adds up to a jolting and haunting
piece of fiction. (Francis M. Nevins, Jr.)

John Lutz. *The Shadow Man.* Morrow, 1981, 215 pp., $10.95.

Each of the crime novels of John Lutz takes off from its
own distinctive premise and develops like nothing he's written
before, and his sixth and latest book is no exception. U.S.
Senator Jerry Andrews is visited in Washington by a college
classmate, a psychiatrist investigating the multiple personalities of the psychotic who assassinated a presidential candi-
date several years ago. There have been hints that one or more
of the killer's identities is able at will to leave the maximum-
security asylum where he's committed--and that he may be out to
kill certain people with whom his various personalities were
involved before the murder. Then the psychiatrist is found
drowned in the Hudson, and Andrews rather implausibly puts his
senatorial duties on indefinite hold, comes to New York incog-
nito to play detective, and is soon stalked through Manhattan's
streets by what may well be an assassin with the power to be in
several places at once.

Although one subtle and almost fair clue presages the book's
ultimate nature, the avalanche of surprise disclosures in the
last fifteen pages may leave readers thinking they've stumbled
into a different story altogether. Even before that point one
or two developments are a bit predictable and a few others hard
to swallow. But the basic situation is stimulating, the pacing
taut, the hints that we are all potential schizoids disturbing,
and the climax in which Andrews and his girl friend are be-
seiged in an isolated Colorado cabin and chased down icy moun-
tain roads by a team of skiing hit men is the most exciting
sequence Lutz has ever written. *The Shadow Man* is not the
author's best but it's briskly readable, totally professional,
and not to be missed by any devotee of suspense. (Francis M.
Nevins, Jr.)

Patrick McGinley. *Bogmail.* Ticknor & Fields, 1981, 259 pp.,
$9.95.

The lady looked the same and the clutter looked the same. The only differences were that the office was smaller and had moved a few blocks.

Soon after the end of World War II, a petite young woman named Joan Kahn joined the New York publisher Harper & Brothers and took over as editor of the firm's line of detective novels, or, as she preferred to call them, novels of crime and suspense. She made it her business to find new blood, to publish writers who would get away from the formulas of drab prose and flat people and stock settings and artificial plots that typified traditional detective fiction at its worst. She hunted for authors who could create character and atmosphere and emotion and who could write as vividly as any mainstream novelist while still telling good, suspenseful stories. The people she published over the next third of a century--Nicholas Blake, Julian Symons, Shelley Smith, Patricia Highsmith, Andrew Garve, Michael Gilbert, Maurice Procter, and Dick Francis, to name just a few --were in the forefront of the movement from the old-style detective story to the contemporary crime novel. Eventually Kahn's prestige led to her own name being prominently featured on all the books she edited. But in recent years Harper, like some other houses, seemed to abandon its commitment to mystery fiction in the lust for blockbuster bestsellers, and a year ago a dispirited Kahn resigned. She is now editing for the new firm of Ticknor & Fields, and her office in that company's Vanderbilt Avenue suite is as full of inspired disorder as her old headquarters at Harper. There she sits, half-buried in manuscripts, a tiny, elfin-voiced lady who smiles and bobs and bookchats in that rapid-fire elliptical way that's uniquely hers as she starts over.

The first new writer to have a John Kahn Book published by Ticknor & Fields is Patrick McGinley, whose *Bogmail* is a fine specimen of mainstream novelistic strengths with relatively weak links to the mystery genre. The setting is a tiny village on the wild northwest coast of Ireland, and the chief character is impotent intellectual pubkeeper Tim Roarty, who bludgeons his daughter's seducer to death with a volume of the 1911 *Encyclopedia Britannica* and disposes of the body in a nearby bog. When he starts receiving extortion letters from an apparent witness to the burial who signs himself Bogmailer, Roarty has the double problem of keeping his crime concealed from the police and finding out (and then killing) the unknown person who saw where the body was buried. At which point the dead man's frozen foot is found hanging from the door knocker of the police station....

McGinley evokes magnificently the wildness of the Donegal landscape, the look and feel and smell of the bogs and the sea, the crude and unbearably lonely village lives, the Irishman's love of talk and more talk as if words could ease the pain of the world, the interplay of a small number of very real people in a supremely vivid environment. But the crime-suspense elements are on stage only intermittently, and at the end, when blind chance has revealed the Bogmailer's identity, we never learn where in that tiny hamlet he managed to keep the corpse frozen yet unfindable by the police. In the microcosm of this novel we can see both what was lost and what was gained in the evolution from traditional to contemporary crime fiction.

The lady hasn't changed and her taste hasn't changed. Under whatever publisher, John Kahn Books will never disappoint

those who insist that a mystery must have before all else the
strengths of any good novel. (Francis M. Nevins, Jr.)

John Ball. *Trouble for Tallon*. Doubleday, 1981, 179 pp.,
$9.95.

John Ball is best known for his books about black homicide
investigator Virgil Tibbs, the sleuth played by Sidney Poitier
in *In the Heat of the Night*, but most of his recent novels have
been about other detectives. In *Police Chief* (1977) Ball introduced Jack Tallon, who resigned from the Pasadena police
department to command an eight-officer force in the small city
of Whitewater, Washington. Tallon earns his badge as a series
character in this second adventure.
The murder of a much-disliked city councilman, who had been
waging a moralistic vendetta against a community of yoga devotees
in geodesic domes not far from Whitewater, forces Tallon to
turn his entire department into part-time plainclothes detectives. The case brings romance to one of the officers, who
falls in love with a movie star searching for inner peace, and
on-the-job training to the entire force as they cope with a
lying deathbed accusation, an ankh stolen from a corporate lawyer turned holy man, a bearded arsonist on a motorcycle, and a
plot to turn the spiritual community into a gambling resort.
The story's threads come together after an excellent night
chace sequence and the arrest of a not too surprising Least
Likely Suspect for murder.
Most of John Ball's mystery novels interweave meticulous
police procedure, deductive detection, and a sedate romance between one of the investigators and a woman in the case, and
Trouble for Tallon is very much in this tradition. The detection element unfortunately is quite weak: the reason the victim
accused innocent persons on his deathbed is never made clear,
the deductions at the climax make little sense, and an officer
is required to act like an idiot so that the killer isn't ex-
posed early in the game by simple legwork. But readers who
want to enter a world where characters live by a code of pro-
priety, restraint, and efficient teamwork, where every policeman is a walking angel, where dialogue and manners are formal
to the point of courtliness, where procedure is exactly what
the rulebook says it is, will enjoy this novel immensely. His
books are worlds removed from the garish and hideous realities
one finds in the novels of Joseph Wambaugh, but John Ball has
no peers in that subgenre that on its face seems impossible,
the *restful* police story. (Francis M. Nevins, Jr.)

Margaret Truman. *Murder in the White House*. Popular Library,
1981, $2.95.

It has been suggested that the Truman opus was ghostwritten;
if so, Miss Truman got the worst of the bargain. The style is
journalistic and masculine, and one gets the impression that
this pedestrian affair was written by a man.
Although Miss Truman has out a new book--*Murder on Capitol
Hill*--one recalls her foray into the music world and the
thought occurs that this second book may mark *finis* to another
brief career. One is also reminded of the short-lived mystery-
writing efforts of Gypsy Rose Lee, whose two books *were* ghosted

by her close friend, the clever Craig Rice. The difference here is that the Lee/Rice pairing produced two salty and funny books. The interesting partnership lasted only through two mysteries, probably because the themes of murder/burlesque quickly were exhausted and because Miss Rice was too busy writing books under her own name.

Among Miss Truman's non-fiction books is one called *Women of Courage*, a title apropos Miss Truman's mystery writing-- definitely *not* her forte.

Margaret Truman knows her way around the White House and all about corruption in high places. But a tour of the White House is not sufficient to hold one's interest, and corruption in high places is too well known to be of much shock value. The plot concerns the murder of the Secretary of State in a tight security area of the White House. This narrows the possible suspects to four, with two already eliminated in readers' minds. The *one* clue, given early on, points directly to the killer. An experienced reader will pick up on it immediately. Thus, the denouement when it comes is neither surprising nor satisfying.

The Characters, except for an interesting parody on Daddy Truman (and Bess?), are cardboard. But then so are the people from whom the characters are drawn--paper dolls foisted upon us every election year. A nude dancer-prostitute comes across well (Miss *Truman!*), ditto an amoral female, Martha Kingsley (Martha Mitchell?), but the lovers are hollow and unconvincing. The dialogue reads just real enough to be *dull*. A little poetic fancy should have helped the text immeasurably.

A gussied up paperback cover, coupled with the Truman name, has hyped the price to $2.95. The same book, penned by a lesser-known personality, might have retailed for much less. VERDICT: Overpriced, overrated, and underdone. (Billy Barton)

Elizabeth Peters. *The Love Talker*. Dodd, Mead, 1980.

With her tongue tucked firmly into her cheek, Elizabeth Peters (Barbara L. Mertz, who also writes as Barbara Michaels) has produced another of her contemporary romantic-suspense stories, *The Love Talker*, and this novel is as enjoyable as its predecessors. The book exploits the current popular interest in fairies and the perennial appeal of the fairy tale. Also, some of the conventions of the gothic are apparent. There is, for instance, the usual large, opulent house, Idlewood, set this time on a Maryland hilltop, and inhabited by a mildly eccentric trio of the senior members of the Morton family, old settlers of the area. As is also often the case in the gothic, the weather is important, this time lending plot complications in the form of ice and snow and enhancing the setting with some really lovely descriptions of nature's flora, fauna, storm, and silence. Another familiar gothic note is the fact that the heroine is pursued by several suitors of varying degrees of attractiveness and acceptability. Both the fairy tale and the gothic influences are at times modified, inverted, or gently spoofed.

The heroine is "a nice big girl named Laura" of the "rosy cheeks and nut-brown hair and three dimples, one in one cheek and two in the other." Cute--but not too cute, for Laura is capable, clever, and, when provoked, sharp-tongued. Laura is

busy working on her doctoral dissertation and dealing with a
failed love affair when annoyance at Chicago winters, fury with
her lover, and a muted call for help from her great-aunt send
her back to Maryland, where bad weather doesn't daunt her and
danger only inspires her.

The problem is that while the elder Mortons are comfortable
financially and aided in their advanced old age by their stunningly handsome, charmingly affable, and unfailingly able handy-
man, Jefferson Banes, Great-aunt Ida has begun to fear for the
sanity of her sister, Elizabeth. Lizzie, always a bit fey, has
become convinced that there are living, active fairies on the
place and has endangered herself while pursuing them. Because
Great-uncle Ned is a love but not a man of practical action,
Aunt Ida appeals to Laurie and her half-brother, Douglas Wright.
Both respond and both soon become convinced that there is a
plot against Lizzie's life.

A cast of well established but undeveloped characters em-
bellishes Laurie and Doug's search for the solution to the mystery. The Schotts, who have grown children thought--by all but
Doug and Laurie--to be perfect mates for the young Mortons,
lend a bit of pale comedy. Also important are the Wilsons,
whose repressed young daughters have provided Lizzie with
photographs of the fairies. The Wilsons are tenants on Morton
land, and Mr. Wilson is a religious fanatic who imposes fierce
(and sometimes violent) restrictions on his children. These
families are the source of subplot, complication, and motivation.

There is only one *idea* in *The Love Talker*, and it is certainly not at all new to mystery-suspense fans: People Are Not
What They Seem. Another limiting factor is Peters' difficulty
with Laura. Clearly, the author is trying for a portrait of a
brisk, independent, assertive young woman, and, also clearly,
that is what the plot demands. But Peters, like all gothic
writers, also seems to need to preach that males are dominant,
and the result is rather fuzzy, stunted characterization.
Nevertheless, *The Love Talker* is pleasant and good fun. The
suspense mounts but never terrifies; the characters perform but
never grow; the climax is a bit arbitrary but well within the
standard pattern. The novel is an entertainment and, in its
way, successful. (Jane S. Bakerman)

Anna Clarke. *This Downhill Path*. McKay-Washburn, 1977.

The protagonist of *This Downhill Path* (published in England
as *The Deathless and the Dead*, 1976) is John Broome, an Oxford
graduate student working on a book about Emily Witherington, a
minor Victorian poet. Touchy about his lower-class background,
John is determined to make a name for himself among literary
scholars, and he firmly believes that his study of Emily's life
and work is his passport to academic success and security.

But ambition is not John's only motivation; he loves literature and is genuinely besotted with the slender poetic output
of Emily's short life (as a very young woman, she was killed
during a wild bicycle ride down Boar's Hill). John also loves
Alice Heron, a wealthy young woman who has moved away from her
domineering family to try to achieve an independent, self-
sufficient life. Because Alice loves John as truly as he loves
her, she offers him what may prove to be special insight for

his work. Sir Roderick and Lady "Belle" Heron, Alice's great
uncle and aunt, the people who reared her, were, as young
people, acquaintances of Emily Witherington. John and Alice
hope that Sir Roderick will be able to provide some hitherto
unknown scraps of information about Emily's life and circle.

The young people plan to keep their affection for one another hidden, but it immediately becomes apparent that there
is more than one secret in the Heron household. Sir Roderick
and his wife, for instance, carry on fierce sniper warfare
which seems to have defined their relationship for years.
Belle Heron has a packet of old letters written by Emily Witherington, and she stealthily passes -hem on to John--to be
read after Lady Heron's death. Those letters are also a key
to the schemes of Miss Letty Mann, the Herons' "lady help," who
has a yen for Sir Roderick--until she faces him in the grip of
one of his terrifying rages. Ultimately, it seems clear to
John that Emily was murdered, that the letters are an important
clue--and that contemporary lives may well be in danger. He
feels compelled to solve these mysteries, though doing so may
well ruin his relationship with Alice.

There are plots within plots in this quiet novel--and yet
there is little physical action. Even the chase sequence is
actually devoted to polite, mannered, conversational dueling.
Nevertheless, the novel is compelling and holds the reader's
interest. The characters are complex and intriguing; almost no
one is exactly what he or she appears, at first glance, to be.
The past shadows the present, and the truth, when it is revealed, makes very real changes in the lives of John and Alice,
for the downhill path traced in this novel is not only Boar's
Hill; it also stands for the disintegration of personalities
and dreams.

This Downhill Path is not for readers devoted to thrills
and chills, but those who relish speculation--and an occasional
shudder--will like it. (Jane S. Bakerman)

Dorothy Simpson. *The Night She Died.* Charles Scribner's Sons,
    1981, 188 pp.

Dorothy Simpson's *The Night She Died* is an excellent example of the British district-outside-of-London mystery. Detective Inspector Luke Thanet's investigation of a stabbing
centers in the town of Sturrendon but also penetrates nearby
villages so that Thanet's manor seems both extensive and vivid.

The stunningly beautiful Julie Holmes has been killed just
inside the front door of her rather secluded home. Her husband, shocked almost into immobility, is a major suspect, as
are her womanizing boss and a glamorous former suitor. One of
the quirks in Julie's character which seems important in the
case is her allure; men are keenly responsive to her, even
though she seems to have been an aloof, fairly unresponsive
person.

Thanet attributes her coolness to psychological damage
stemming from the fact that Julie witnessed another murder as
a tiny child, and the policeman becomes convinced that Julie's
killer is the same person who committed the unsolved crime in
the past. Accordingly, he devotes a good deal of time and
energy to investigating the earlier death, despite the skepti-
cism of his aide, Detective Sergeant Mike Lineham.

Lineham is a promising investigator, but he is a bit too diffident. There is some good byplay when Lineham, at Thanet's urging, begins to speak out a little--and despite himself, Thanet becomes annoyed. The relationship between the two men is intriguing and has lots of potential.

Thanet's family life (he has a pleasant wife, Joan, and two small children, Bridget and Ben) also contributes to the interest of the novel. Clearly, the couple are devoted to one another, and the inspector consciously tries to protect their marriage from some of the stresses generated by his job. His scenes with Bridget are appealing and not cloying.

Generally speaking, then, Simpson has assembled some standard ingredients--an attractive, specific area, a right-hand man who generates tension as well as aid, and an appealing personal background for her capable, if not infallible, protagonist. Despite the familiarity of these factors, Simpson's touch is fresh and sure.

There is one flaw, however. Simpson strives for realism in her conclusion, and to some degree she achieves it. The problem is that to do so she resorts to contrivance rather than genuine development. Nevertheless, the novel works very well; it's a sound piece of work. (Jane S. Bakerman)

Catherine Aird. *A Late Phoenix*. Bantam Books, 1981, 164 pp.

The opening days of Dr. William Latimer's new practice in Berebury form the frame for one of the most interesting cases of Detective Inspector C.D. Sloan who, once again, works with the irritating Detective Constable Crosby. As usual, Sloan proceeds with imagination and empathy; Crospy proceeds.

Latimer's surgery is located in the St. Luke's section of the town, and the first steps are being taken to convert the World War II bomb site opposite into rental property. As the construction workers begin clearing the site, a skeleton is uncovered. Pathology reports reveal that the bones belong to a young woman who was pregnant--and murdered. Sloan is faced with the task of identifying the corpse and solving the dated but still open case. Grim proof that the case is still very current appears when another murder takes place and a third is finally revealed.

During the war, of course, Sloan was a child, and much of the interest of the novel arises from his dim memories, the comments of people who were adults during the early forties, and the inspector's efforts to inform himself of the procedures followed during the blitz, for the devastation in the area has been used to mask the original crime.

Aird uses this history lesson--attractively and enticingly presented--as a king of auxiliary detection project in this novel. Sloan seeks the past as vigorously as he seeks the killer. Latimer's story, of course, offers further embellishment, as do the glimpses of the Sloans' family life.

All these extra factors are all to the good, for while the case itself is carefully detailed, while incidental characterizations are neatly drawn, and while the clues *are*, in fact, planted, the conclusion is a bit strained, a bit contrived. *A Late Phoenix* is well worth reading, though. As usual, Catherine Aird does a neat, careful job, and Sloan comes ever more convincingly alive, even though the killer does not. (Jane S. Bakerman)

Anne Morice. *Death in the Round*. St. Martin's Press, 1981, 192 pp.

When Tessa Crichton, actress and amateur sleuth, takes a job at the Deerhaven, Dorset, Rotunda Theatre, murder, not very surprisingly, follows. Elfrieda Henshaw, the highly regarded repertory theater's owner, has invested much of her life in the company, and her devotion has overcome age, illness, and financial pressures right up until her violent death. Elfrieda's most recent obsession, Melanie, a tough, flamboyant, teenaged orphan, has become the bane of the Rotunda's staff, and their responses to her, her schemes, and to one another generate the plot's complications, as does a second killing.

As far as many of the other members of the company are concerned, Tessa herself is often another complication. The actress is pushy, acerbic, nosey, bright, determined, curious--and often quite right in her deductions. Much of her sleuthing involves extended conversations in the course of which motives aplenty are revealed. These rather mannered chats also reveal a cast of interesting characters--especially Tessa's landlady, Viola, a fellow actress and compulsive pourer of oil upon troubled waters, and their neighbor, Jamie Crother, a playwright who does needlework for relaxation and keeps a supply of champagne at Viola's cottage where he stitches and sips when he feels the need of human companionship.

Despite the reluctance of her fellow actors, Tessa perseveres and unmasks the killer, and, though the solution may not surprise careful readers, they will find *Death in the Round* a neat, workmanlike job. As usual, Anne Morice proves herself a capable writer. Fans will find exactly what they expect; new readers will meet an independent, determined protagonist. (Jane S. Bakerman)

Robert B. Parker. *Looking for Rachel Wallace*. Delacorte, 1980.

Up to now I haven't read a good thing about this novel, and I haven't read much in favour of Mr. Parker for a couple of years or more. Which surprises me, because I enjoyed the book (as I did its predecessor, the much maligned *Judas Goat*) and found that the things I've always enjoyed about Parker were in evidence once again. Wise-cracking Spenser and his equally urbane lady love (if he gets tired of her she can come to me any time), some nicely handled action scenes, and a well-painted portrait of the forceful, intelligent feminist lesbian whose protection is Spenser's latest assignment. He gets kicked off the case (by Rachel Wallace) and then goes back to it because she is kidnapped and he may be the only one who can save her. The plot isn't as devious as some I've come across, and Spenser isn't (and never has been) as introspective and self-doubting as Marlowe--but that's because he's Spenser, not Marlowe, and what's wrong with that? (Bob Adey)

Thomas Berger. *Who Is Teddy Villanova?* Eyre Methuen, 1977.

A pastiche (for this is what I take this private eye novel to be) is difficult to maintain for more than short story length, so all in all the author doesn't do so badly at all

with this incredibly complicated, closely written tale of p.i.
Russell Wren (obligatorily ex-English literature teacher) and
his unwitting involvement in what seems to start as a shadowy
feud between two equally shadowy figures, Teddy Villanova and
Junior Washburn. The solution is as plausible as one could
expect, the writing hugely enjoyable in parts. (Bob Adey)

Lionel Black. *The Penny Murders*. Avon, 1980.

I came to this book because I was tipped off (quite correctly) that there was a locked room murder in it. I hoped
also that husband and wife sleuths Kate and Henry Theobald
might become old friends--but I'm afraid that won't be so.
After the first twenty pages I had already found the characters
and situations so completely artificial and uninteresting that
I gave it up. A pity, because the locked room gimmick is quite
neat and a new one on me. Can't win 'em all. (Bob Adey)

V.C. Clinton-Baddeley. *My Foe Outstretch'd Beneath the Tree*.
Dell/Murder Ink Mystery, 1981, $2.25.

V.C. Clinton-Baddeley introduced his retired Oxford don/
detective, Dr. Davie, in *Death's Bright Dart* (1967). *My Foe*,
first published in 1968, is the second in the series. I don't
know why it has taken me so long to encounter Dr. Davie, but I
am pleased that the introduction has finally been made, and
dismayed that there are only four other titles in which to con-
tinue the acquaintance. (The others in the series are *Only a
Matter of Time* [1969], *No Case for the Police* [1970], and the
posthumously published *To Study a Long Silence* [1972].)
One of the main joys of the book is the prose: cool, literate, and infused with a quiet and puckish wit. Dr. Davie's
intellect is also quiet and puckish, but no less acute for
being understated. He possesses broad knowledge in many areas,
a lively curiosity, an understanding of human nature and motivations, and the true detective's ability to penetrate to the
essentials of a tangle of facts and to make connections among
seemingly unrelated circumstances.
The circumstances include the murder of Morris Brent, an
ex-policeman, perennial bully, and all-around unpleasant character, who somehow had managed to become a member of the exclusive Chesterfield Club--on the grounds of which he is, one
morning, discovered "outstretch'd beneath the tree," having
been knocked unconscious and then smothered. Along with the
mystery of Brent's demise, the plot involves strange goings-on
at a girls' college (where Dr. Davie delivers a lecture on
"Irony in Poetry"), the oddities of a tape-recorded correspon-
dence course in English-for-foreigners, and a suburban London
production of *Manon Lescaut*. All of these threads are drawn
together in satisfying fashion, thanks to Dr. Davie's acute-
ness. A cast of well-limned supporting characters adds an
extra touch of flavor to a very enjoyable tale. (R.E. Briney)

Charlotte MacLeod. *The Luck Runs Out*. Avon, 1981, $2.25;
originally published by Doubleday, 1979.

I like this even more than I did the first book about Peter Shandy and the goings-on at Balaclava Agricultural College. One reason may be the larger role played by the college president, Thorkjeld Svenson--now there's a man who knows how a college should be run! Shandy has lost or redirected some of the maverick spirit that led to the manic Christmas display in *Rest You Merry*, but this is more than balanced by the gain of a wife, Helen Marsh from the earlier book. This time the crimes include the theft of a stock of gold from an exclusive gold- and silversmith establishment, the Carlovingian Crafters; the pignapping of Belinda of Balaclava, an 853-pound pregnant sow of inestimable emotional and financial value to the college; and the brutal murder of Martha Flackley, the elderly woman who served as farrier to the College's horses. Shandy's investigations involve him with the usual mix of eccentric faculty, scarcely less eccentric students, and assorted visitors. In a climactic and all-to-brief hand-to-hand battle, Shandy and Thorkjeld Svenson capture the villains and save the College's bacon, in more ways than one. A witty and well-plotted delight. (R.E. Briney)

Henry Cecil. *Tell You What I'll Do*. Simon and Schuster, 1970.

When I mentioned to a friend that I was reading a book by Henry Cecil, the friend replied, "Oh, yes, he writes funny books about judges and lawyers."
Indeed he does. Also about confidence tricksters, clergymen, retired army colonels, female cousins, and shoplifters. The present book involves all of these types. The central character, an amiable and goodhearted fellow named Harry Woodstock, is a specialist in the "long firm" gambit. ("No violence and no blackmail," said Harry. "Those are my rules and I stick to them. Just honest to God fraud.") For reasons of his own, he finds it expedient to spend long periods in jail. His efforts to arrange these sojourns, and the contrary efforts of a prison chaplain to reform him, are the nominal concern of the book. This light plot is, however, merely a frame for the display of the author's specialty: a succession of memorably antic conversations and mad courtroom scenes.
The writer of the jacket copy, mindful of his intended audience--the book is presented as an Inner Sanctum Mystery--felt obliged to promise the reader a suspenseful story with a hair-raising and ingenious denouement. A reviewer of the original British edition was more accurate, calling up echoes of Waugh, Wodehouse, and the early Alec Guinness comedies. The book is not long on action, mystery, or suspense. It is simply very, very funy. (R.E. Briney, reprinted from *The Mystery Reader's Newsletter*, April, 1970.)

P.M. Hubbard. *The Dancing Man*. Atheneum, 1971.

This novel, the author's ninth, displays a remarkable unity of theme, locale, and execution. A certain aspect of archaeology is made the motive for a crime (which may or may not be murder); the setting is an as yet undeveloped site of great archaeological significance (and what this significance is becomes apparent only gradually); and the narration itself is structured like an archaeological investigation--layer after

layer of the past is peeled away and analyzed, until the truth
comes to light.

Mark Hawkins receives word that his younger brother, an
archaeologist specializing in neolithic Britain, has disappeared
during a visit to a colleague in the west of England. The pre-
sumption is that he was accidentally killed while on one of his
solitary rock-climbing excursions, but no body has been found.
Mark visits his brother's erstwhile host and immediately becomes involved in a tangle or relationships with the three odd
members of the household: the historian and archaeologist Roger
Merrion, his wife Ethel, at once passionate and remote, and his
remarkable sister Cynthia. But the physical setting soon over-
shadows the people: the lonely house surrounded by the brooding
wood, the standing stone with its phallic carving (the "dancing
man:), the oddly repellent ruins of a Cistercian abbey nearby,
and the immensely older and more threatening ruins underneath.
Mark finds that all of these contribute to the elucidation of
the mystery of his brother's disappearance. In the climactic
episode, he must undertake the almost superhuman task of rais-
ing single-handedly a gigantic fallen monolith. The interplay
between the practical engineering problem and the strange atmosphere which has been building throughout the book is admir-
ably done. In the end, the present proves more deadly than the
past.

In setting and mood, and in the use of survivals from British prehistory, *The Dancing Man* calls up faint echoes of some
of Arthur Machen's tales of terror. However, calm reason pre-
vails, and the preternatural is kept on the fringes, so understated that the reader may choose not to notice it. But if one
does ignore it, what a waste of those fine concluding lines!
(R.E. Briney, reprinted from *The Mystery Reader's Newsletter*,
July/August 1971.)

Laurence Oriol [Noëlle Loriot]. *Short Circuit*. Belmont Books,
1971; translated from the French by W.G. Corp.

A reviewer for the London *Times* invoked comparison with the
works of Agatha Christie in reviewing the British edition of
this book, a translation of *L'Interne de Service*, winner of the
Grand Prix de Littérature Policière in 1966. The reference is
exaggerated, but not entirely inappropriate. Certainly the
central subject is one which Mrs. Christie has treated on numerous occasions: the small group of people whose ingrown personal relationships lead inexorably to murder. Here we are
presented with Guillaume Brassart, the distinguished but aging
surgeon; his clever and demanding mistress, Danielle; his bored
wife, Louise, to whom social disgrace is the ultimate threat;
and the young intern, Vincent Debosse, drawn into the lives of
the other three for reasons which he does not understand. It
soon becomes clear that any of the four could have a motive for
murdering any of the others. And from this derives the prin-
cipal suspense of the book. For, although the corpse is discovered, electrocuted in bed, on the first page, we do not
learn the identity of the victim until near the end of the
book. The bulk of the novel is occupied by a flashback which
chronicles the events leading up to the crime: the cross-cur-
rents of selfishness and passion, and the grotesque murder plot
which they generate. Will it succeed? Or will it back-fire?

With novels of this caliber, Belmont can do much to refurbish its somewhat tarnished image. Prime candidates for reprinting, if English translations were available, would be Mlle. Loriot's two previous mystery novels, *A Coeur Ouvert* (1963) and *La Chasse aux Innocents* (1965). Let us hope that we will not be deprived of these indefinitely. (R.E. Briney, reprinted from *The Mystery Reader's Newsletter*, September/October 1971.)

Frank McAuliffe. *The Bag Man*. Zebra, 1979, 192 pp.

I wonder if the Frank McAuliffe who wrote this book is the same man who write the very different (and thoroughly excellent Augustus Mandress series for Ballantine several years ago? If so, he has certainly changed his style and his subject. The Bag Man, Cord, specializes in laundering money for the Mob, and the complicated procedure he follows involves more twists and turns and more suitcases than *What's up Doc?* His usual job is made more difficult this time by the fact that the Don for whom he works is being held prisoner by some rotten types who want both to take over the Don's territory and get their hands on the two million dollars that Cord is shuttling around the country. Cord, however, wants to hang onto the money and rescue the Don. It all makes an interesting story, told in a style slightly reminiscent of Richard Stark's Parker series, terse and straightforward. Good reading if you like that sort of thing. (Bill Crider)

Walter Wager. *Blue Leader*. Berkley, 1981; first published by Arbor House, 1979.

The paperback edition of *Blue Leader* boasts a McGinnis cover, and that alone might encourage some people to buy it. There is also a blurb which tells us that the book is the first in a series featuring A.B. Gordon, "The sexiest Private Eye who ever packed a .357 Magnum." Don't be misled by the blurb. Alison Gordon is a detective, all right, and the book begins like it might be a p.i. story; but it's not. After about forty-seven pages, the book turns into one of those "private army *vs.* the opium smugglers" things with the usual elements: recruiting the team, training the team, the hit, and so on. A.B. Gordon of course turns out to be a former CIA operative who fits right into the scheme. There are a few nice touches--the mission requires B-17s and B-17 pilots, for one thing--but Modesty Blaise does this sort of job much better. (Bill Crider)

Anthony Boucher. *The Seven of Calvary*. Simon & Shuster, 1937.

Boucher's place in mystery criticism and mystery fandom is well established. His own efforts at writing in the field, however, are sadly difficult to locate. When read, it is with a mixture of disappointment and enjoyment. The disappointment comes from the characterization, or lack of it. Martin Lamb is the protagonist here. He is studying German and Sanskrit at the University of California at Berkeley. He lives at International House with an assortment of other students, professors, and assistants from around the world. Unfortunately, most of the other residents and students remain flat and undifferentiated. They never come alive.

The good parts predominate. There is a puzzle and Boucher plays fair with the reader. Martin's friend and mentor, Dr. Ashwin, serves as an admirable armchair detective, fed information on the crime by Martin. The academic setting and literate conversation are enjoyable but not overly pretentious or dry. There is also a minor theatrical theme, revolving around the school's production of a play that Martin translated from Spanish. The dress rehearsal of the play is a pivotal scene in the unfolding of the mystery.

The best thing about *Calvary* is the solution. I'll say no more about it, but it is uncommon yet logical (and not, admittedly, unique). It has an extra poetic justice twist that I particularly liked. If Boucher had been able to develop his characters with the same skill he showed in plotting and cohesive writing he could be as commonly known as Queen and Gardner. (Fred Dueren)

Lucille Kallen. *Introducing C.B. Greenfield* and *C.B. Greenfield: The Tanglewood Murder*. Ballantine, 1979 and 1980.

Kallen's engaging detective duo is off to a snappy start. Reporter Maggie Rome and newspaper editor C.B. Greenfield are direct descendants of the '30s and '40s detective teams of friendly antagonists. Maggie reminds me most of Grace Latham--rather independent, resourceful, intelligent, with a family of grown sons and a husband lurking in the background. But Maggie is a modern heroine. She does not keep things from Charlie (C.B.), at least not intentionally, and she doesn't run off on her own to explore creaky houses in the middle of a midnight storm.

Greenfield, on the other hand, is most reminiscent of Nero Wolfe (and Maggie makes an admirable foe in their continuous repartee). Charlie has the essential self-centeredness, a fondness for extravagant words, and is something of a gourmet. But the banter and digs, the one-upmanship, and the threats of quitting are strong reminders. Unfortunately for Maggie, she has yet to get in the last word.

Introducing is the better of the two books. It creates the small-town world of Sloan's Ford in New York. As reporter and owner/editor/ publisher of the weekly newspaper, Maggie and Charlie know twelve-year-old Peter Kittell, a delivery boy. Just after buying a ten-speed bicycle with his savings, Peter is struck by a hit-and-run driver and lands in the hospital in a coma. Charlie's determination to find the driver sends Maggie out as investigator. She is soon embroiled with the well-to-do Hollis family and learning things about the townspeople she'd rather not know. Then one of the family members disappears, and the only traces are an abandoned Mercedes and a bloody metal fence post left beside the river.

In *The Tanglewood Murder* the newspaper is on vacation and Charlie is set to go up to the Tanglewood music concerts. As a classical music lover--and provider of transportation--Maggie is drug along. But all is not going well with the Boston Symphony Orchestra during rehearsals. Mysterious, annoying incidents occur, provoking nervous apprehension among the musicians.

Murder enters when one of the violinists dies during practice.
Charlie coordinates Maggie's investigations, bringing about a
surprise, if not fully prepared for, ending.

The strong point of both books is the liveliness of the
characters. Maggie and Charlie are as real as your next door
neighbors and probably more interesting. Greenfield should be
able to settle in for a long run. (Fred Dueren)

Eugene Franklin. *Murder Trapp*. Stein and Day, 1971.

The detective is named Berkeley H. Barnes; the source of
his name is explained in these terms:

> The name may sound pretentious, but his parents had nothing of the
> sort in mind. His mother had been reading Bishop Berkeley's *A New
> Theory of Vision* during the last weeks of her pregnancy and became
> sort of convinced the whole thing was an illusion. Consequently,
> when Berkeley H. arrived, she was in a Chinese restaurant calmly
> trying to decide which one from the "A" list and which two from
> the "B" list. His entry into the world was assisted by a Chinese
> waiter who had had some experience as a midwife. Not many people
> know that the H in his name stands for Hoy.

The potential victim is Hammersmith Trapp, head of a large Madison Avenue advertising agency, who hires Barnes to discover
who has been making attempts on his life (such as a rusty car-
pet tack smeared with horse manure and placed in the cushion
of Trapp's chair, to give him a fatal case of lockjaw) and to
ensure that future attempts are not successful. There are
characters named Shunk and Tertius Carraway and Isabel Bell and
Unser Z. Weser and Corfan Greenhouse and ....

From the punning title to the funny names, quirky characters, clever dialogue, and absurd situations, this apparently
first novel by the pseudonymous Mr. Franklin is so resolutely
"comic" that it made my teeth itch. (R.E. Briney, reprinted
from *The Mystery Reader's Newsletter*, September/October 1971).

S.H. Courtier. *Ligny's Lake*. Simon & Schuster, 1971.

Sandy Carmichael and Lewis Ligny were little more than casual acquaintances; they had met only because Ligny was a neighbor of Sandy's brother-in-law in suburban Canberra. Still,
Sandy was puzzled and hurt when he was rudely snubbed by Ligny
at a boxing-match in Melbourne--and the puzzlement became in-
credulity less than an hour later when Sandy learned from the
late news on TV that Lewis Ligny had disappeared--apparently
drowned while swimming early that same morning near Canberra,
almost five hundred miles from Melbourne.... The encounter at
the boxing-match could hardly have been a case of mistaken
identity, for Ligny's appearance was quite distinctive: his
face was badly scarred and deformed, a result of wartime in-
juries about which he never spoke. Sandy determines to search
for the truth. His clues include the boxing-match, Ligny's
elaborate hobby (a miniature engineering complex in which scale
models of trains, cars, and ships travelled around and across
an oddly shaped artificial lake), a stolen copy of *Walden*. His
only ally in the search is eighty-one-year-old Miss Rhoda Han-

cock, whose past is somehow linked to that of Lewis Ligny. In spite of opposition from Australian Security and, astonishingly, from Sandy's own family, he perseveres in his search, which leads him eventually to a deserted island in the Tasman Sea. Only the island is not quite deserted....

S.H. Courtier, an Australian school teacher and literary scholar, wrote some twenty-three suspense novels, many of them dealing with the elucidation of a mystery whose roots are buried in the past. *Ligny's Lake* is an admirable variation on this theme. It depends less on purely Australian background than most of the other novels, but this in no way detracts from the charm and effectiveness of the story. Read it. And then join in the search for Courtier's all-too-elusive earlier works. (R.E. Briney, reprinted from *The Mystery Reader's Newsletter*, September/October 1971).

Keith Laumer. *Deadfall*. Doubleday/Crime Club, 1971.

Keith Laumer is a prolific and popular writer of science fiction adventure novels, known for solid plotting, headlong action, and an often vivid and evocative prose style. What a pity that so little of his undoubted talent is observable in his debut in the mystery field. He has attempted a "tough, classic detective novel" (the blurb-writer's phrase) in the style of Raymond Chandler, to whom the book is dedicated. Almost every situation and character--starting on page one with the Moose Molloy-figure of Lou Anglich--evokes comparison with a similar element in Chandler. The comparisons are disastrous for *Deadfall*. In trying to hew close to the line of his original, Laumer has in fact chopped his way through to the other side, and produced a book that reads like a Stan Freberg parody. Back to the Galactic Empire! (R.E. Briney, reprinted from *The Mystery Reader's Newsletter*, January/March 1972.)

John Godey. *The Three Worlds of Johnny Handsome*. Random House, 1972.

"Handsome is as handsome does," but can the saying be reversed? Young John Sedley, highly intelligent but incredibly ugly, drifted into crime after years of cruel rejection by "normal" society. Dr. Katsouras, conducting a medical/psychological experiment at the prison where Sedley is an inmate, believes that he can be rehabilitated and given a chance at a productive life by means of cosmetic surgery to correct his deformities. But will improvements in outward form lead to corresponding alterations in behavior?

John Godey provides no convincing general arguments one way or the other; he simply picks his answer and explores its inevitable consequences. He creates ample sympathy for "Johnny Handsome," but it is generalized and unfocused. We never learn enough about Johnny to understand why he makes the decisions he does. As a result, the book is only superficially and temporarily convincing. But this does not prevent it from being a compelling reading experience: it is no easier to quit this book in the middle than it is to get off a toboggan once it has started downhill.

Sam Peckinpah would love the ending. (R.E. Briney, reprinted from *The Mystery Reader's Newsletter*, n.d. [1972].)

The Documents In the Case

(Letters)

From Al Hubin, 3656 Midland Ave., White Bear Lake, MN 55110:

Robert Samoian's letter in the latest *Mystery Fancier* (Vol 5 #4 was consumed in one sitting with much pleasure and interest) inspires me to finally make of record something that it's long been my intention to get into print.

Samoian listed several publisher's errors in respect to authors' names, and there are several others of that sort which other readers will doubtless supply.

One notable publisher's error of a different kind has, I think, gone completely unremarked, and this is all the more surprising as the author in the case was Arthur Conan Doyle. It stands as a sort of all-time monument to publisher incompetence.

In the early years of this century a Chicago publisher of no particular note, The Henneberry Company, put out an undated (and pirated?) volume called *My Friend the Murderer and Other Mysteries and Adventures*. They clearly grabbed stories from various other places, since the margins and type faces are not the same for all the tales. The volume has no table of contents, but the stories are "My Friend the Murderer," "The Silver Hatchet," "The Gully of Bluemansdyke," "The Parson of Jackman's Gulch," "Cyprian Overbeck Wells," "John Barrington Cowles," "Elias B. Hopkins," and "The Ring of Thoth."

So far, it would seem, so good. But the subtitle to "Elias B. Hopkins" is "The Parson of Jackman's Gulch" and it is identical to the story under that title, though in different typeface. So in its scramble and haste to put the book out, this magnificently blundering publisher included one story twice under two different titles!

From Bill Crider, 4206 Ninth St., Brownwood, TX 76801:

You'll notice that I'm making not a single derogatory remark about your Audie Murphyish appearance this time. Jeez, if you told that story about the WAFs and the Ovaltine, I'd be finished in fandom.

Here's my one comment for this time. In his letter in TMF 5:4, Walter Albert almost volunteers to do a film column. I think you should encourage him, force him, or bribe him to do it. His remark that he's "not sure that there is that much appropriate stuff along the way" just won't hold water. This summer alone has given us enough mystery or mystery-related movies to fill several columns, and Walter sees plenty of old films which he could discuss. Members of DAPA-EM have known for a long time that Walter writes about movies as well as anyone doing reviews for the mass markets, and better than most of them. I know that Walter is busy, but I for one think he should share his talents with a wider audience than the readership of DAPA-EM. Cajole him, threaten him, do what you have to. But get the column. Even if Walter wants to review *The Texas Chainsaw Massacre.* [...]

    P.S. That's not all, after all. Robert Samoian's letter about the spelling of authors' names reminds me that Gold Medal book 195, *Saratoga Mantrap*, is by Dexter St. Clare, while book K1312 is by Dester St. Clair. The latter's title is *The Lady's Not for Living*. And Keith Vining, author of Ace D-1, *Too Hot for Hell*, becomes Keith Vinning on the cover and spine of *A Family Affair* (Newsstand Library, 1961). He remains Vining on the title and copyright pages, however.

From Bob Briney, 4 Forest Ave., Salem, MA 01970:

    "And now for something completely different"--in the recently published *Theodore Sturgeon: A Primary and Secondary Bibliography* by Lahna F. Diskin (G.K. Hall, 1980), item A150 on page 25 reads:

    A150 *The Player on the Other Side* (Ellery Queen, pseud). N.Y.: Random House.

No substantiation, no attribution of the source of the information, but at least the assertion is now out in plain sight, in a library reference book.

    Belated comments on TMF 5:3. Walter Albert's dissection of the Skene Melvin bibliography is appreciated. The omission of the specialized journals such as TAD, *The Mystery Reader's Newsletter*, TMF, *Pen*, etc., is crippling to any claim of comprehensiveness, and the comments on other inadequacies of content are well taken. I am less convinced by the strictures on proper bibliographic style. Accuracy and completeness of information are the essentials, and if they are satisfied, then what matter if some minor violence is done to the MLA Style Sheet (which is, after all, not graven on stone)? Concision for its own sake is not necessarily a virtue, especially when it conceals information: for example, a journal citation such as Walter's ELT 13:203-209 does not indicate the date, which is something that a user of the bibliography might well want to know without having to consult an auxiliary source.

    In his review of Wilson Tucker's *To Keep or Kill*, Steve Lewis implies that the author largely abandoned detective fiction after his fifth Charles Horne novel in 1951. Not quite true. Since then he has published six more non-sf suspense novels, some of which qualify as detective fiction and all of which are noticeably less wacky than the Horne novels. A brand new suspense novel is due this year. (During the same thirty-year period, Tucker published nine science fiction novels, a couple of which won awards, and one collection of sf short stories.)

    Regarding Barry Van Tilburg's comments on the copyright notices in the Fu Manchu books: it is an unfortunate fact (for bibliographers) that such notices in reprint editions simply cannot be taken at face value. The Collier reprints, and those by A.L. Burt, Grosset & Dunlap, McKinlay, Stone & Mackenzie, etc., were usually made from plates supplied by the original publisher, and none of the reprint companies bothered to change the copyright or date information on the reverse of the title page. The "Copyright 1930 by P.F. Collier & Son" refers to the *Collier's* magazine serial, not to the Collier book edition. Such misleading (if not outright false) information in the books themselves has been causing problems for book dealers and collectors for years.

TMF 5:4. A resounding "Yes" to Walter Albert's offer to write a film column. And reviews of non-English critical works. (How easy it is to approve of extra work for other people!) [*Walter, you can't possibly turn down Bill Crider and Bob Briney both.*]

If we are being picky (and why not?), Kenneth Millar's pseudonym on *The Moving Target* was, as Frank Floyd says, just plain John Macdonald. Then he changed to John Ross Macdonald, and finally to Ross Macdonald. Three variations, not two. The easiest way to keep all of the Mac/McD's straight is to spell their last names correctly: Ross is Macdonald, John D. is Mac-Donald, and Gregory is Mcdonald. (This leaves Donald and Hugh and George and Hazel and Philip and Ronald and William to fend for themselves....)

My mouth has already started to water in anticipation of Mike Cook's *Monthly Murders,* even though--from the described size of the volume--it may be necessary to take out a second mortgage in order to afford a copy....

From Martin Morse Wooster, 8906 Talbot, Silver Spring, MD:

Walter Albert will perhaps be surprised to find that I am in agreement with him about damping any discussion about "academic" prose. I've said everything that needs saying about pedantry, and I won't say any more--except that I am not against scholarship, but rather against the tendency of some of your correspondents to act as literary vampires, draining all the juice out of the genre that we love. I find Jane Bakerman, for example, unreadable; her remarks about *A Judgment in Stone* are, well, judgments in stone. (Her citation of her earlier article on Rendell in TMF I find rather funny, in a droll sort of way.)

I'd like to see a film column in TMF, and I hope that Walter writes it. [*Come on, Walter; don't let this dissuade you.*] (I'd volunteer, but I tend to see most of the new crime films--and some of them are indeed crimes--in triple bills.) I would also second Walter's proposed reviews on French critical works. Walter has access to French material that none of the rest of us would ever know about, and an incisive article on French mystery criticism would certainly be a highpoint of a future TMF.

I'd also hope that Bob Adey would review some of the British mystery series that are unlikely to cross over to our shores. I've heard very good reports of such series as *The Professionals* and *Sapphire and Steel,* but insofar as these series aren't period pieces, we're unlikely to see them over here. (The local public-television station, though, is showing *The Omega Factor,* a psychic-investigator/spy series produced by the BBC Scottish service. Good acting as always, but too low-key to be really gripping.)

I've just finished *Tinker, Tailor, Soldier, Spy,* and I disagree with Harry Dawson's criticism of it. Le Carré is more complex than Dawson makes him out to be; le Carré is not just writing about the passage of generations in *Tinker, Tailer*, but rather about the loss of empire, of the reduction of power from Smiley's generation to his successors. Le Carré is a political as well as a social novelist, and the death of Control in *Tinker, Tailor* is a political as well as a social truth. If I were to write an article on Le Carré, I would have explained that le Carré's great distinction as a novelist is his ability to understand the dynamic of bureaucracies, the way that bureaucrats try to cover their world with blankets of indecision. Le Carré's ability to understand the dynamics of government is one reason he is one of the premier novelists (and not just crim novelists) of our time.

From Iwan Hedman, Flodins väg 5, 152 00 Strängnäs, Sweden:
I'll start with an answer to Walter Albert, who suggested my name plus Jacques Baudou in his letter.
As a good friend of E.F. Bleiler I was surprised that he himself hasn't mentioned to me this problem of getting review copies from European publishers. I must say that I have almost no problems at all in getting review copies from England, Italy, Germany, or any other country plus USA. Of course there are some problems with USA as American publishers do not usually send their books to Europe for review purposes, but still there is only one or two books I've failed to get for my DAST. Most publishers are very easy to cooperate with and they send books to DAST on a regular basis.
Anyway, I'll be happy to help both my friend Bleiler and other magazine publishers with review books from Scandinavia. From England I think it's much easier to write directly to the publisher asking for the wanted book. You can write to me and I'll forward your letter to each publisher--and then he can decide what to do with your request.
I especially enjoyed Marvin Lachman's article "It's About Crime." In fact, I have often thought about selling my whole collection of fiction and collecting only non-fiction books in our genre. But it has always stopped just with that thought.
By the way, would you like me to write a short piece on the Crime Writers Third World Congress in Stockholm this June? Just a brief one. Finally, I don't agree with Jeff Banks who wants shorter letter sections. I think that section is one of the most valuable in your mag.
[*I wrote back to Iwan immediately and told him I'd love to have the Crime Writers Congress write-up; it arrived yesterday, too late for this issue, but you'll see it in the next TMF. Thanks, Iwan.*]

From Bob Adey, 7 Highcroft Ave., Wordsley, Stourbridge, West Midlands, DY8 5LX, England:
I grabbed up the latest TMF as it arrived rather like a junkie getting his fix (a very appropriate simile for my book collecting/mystery reading habit, I am told). Another good issue.
I enjoyed Sampson's "Peterman of the Old School," Kelley on Faust, and Billy Barton's delightfully original self-interview. Some of the views expressed quite make me want to buy his book.
Robert Samoian's letter about printing errors--particularly in authors' names: on my shelves right at this moment is Her-

bert Bream's *The Darker the Night* (Heinemann) and Margaret Miller's *The Invisible Worm* (John Long). Perhaps the most interesting one I have is the war-time Gollancz novel *Momentary Stoppage*. My copy (the only one I've ever seen) is in a tattered dust wrapper bearing the author's name A.F. Grey. Imagine my surprise when, idly examining the wrapper, I discovered that on the reverse of it the whole thing was printed again, only the author's name was A.S. Grey. Obviously the extreme paper shortage here during the war would not allow the publisher to scrap the misprinted wrapper, so they simply turned them over and did them again.

From Barry Van Tilburg, 4380-67th Ave. N., Pinellas Park, FL:
   I was in Europe checking out the scenery when TMF 5:3 came. Everyone I saw that wasn't carrying a tourist guidebook had a mystery book in tow. It really warms the heart. I remember an elderly lady in a park in Belgium reading an Agatha Christie, a young man in Schiphol airport reading a Nick Carter, and a Danish gentleman on the plane back reading a Martin Beck book (I think it was *The Terrorists*). My regards to Harry Dawson, John le Carré, and George Smiley. Let's let poor George rest. He has had a rough time. Charlie Muffin has become the new George Smiley. If anybody caught it, sorry about the screw-up about the new James Bond book. Bond didn't trade his Aston Martin in because he drove a Bentley. Did you see the new Bond movie yet? It seems to have bits and pieces of different books in it. He even meets up with his old enemy Blofeld again. With the death of Bernard Lee they had to put poor "M" on holiday and have chief of staff take over. "M" was referred to as Sir Miles Messervy in the book *Colonel Sun* and chief of staff is Bill Tanner. "M" was also called by his real name by Bond in *The Man with the Golden Gun*. *Octopussy* is to be the next movie. I hope it is better than the book. Fleming wrote these stories and put them away in a safe not considering them good enough to publish and if you've read them you will know why.
   [*From a later letter:*] As for Jeff Banks, well, hcw could I outdo a master? His section of *Twentieth Century Crime and Mystery Writers* on these two authors cannot be outdone. As Dirty Harry said in Magnum Force, "a man has to know his limitations." I collect only hardbacks and therefore will stick to the subject that I know most about and the books at my fingertips. I hope people don't think that I consider paperbacks as garbage. I have read all the Atlee, Hamilton, and Carter books. But my favorite paperback series is James Dark's Mark Hood series.

From Jo Ann Vicarel, 2571 Eaton Rd., University Heights, OH:
   After many years of hoping to attend Bouchercon, I find that there is a good chance that I can attend this year. Will you please send me information or the address of the person who is in charge this year, plus information about dates and where it is to be held? [*See the back cover of this issue.*] ...
   [...] I am working on an article on Helen McCloy and one on Barbara Paul. So who knows when, but hopefully this year they will be written. [*Soon, I hope.*]

BoucherCon XII

*(ANNUAL CONVENTION OF MYSTERY WRITERS AND READERS,
WITH GUEST OF HONOR, HELEN McCLOY)*

FAN GUEST OF HONOR ALLEN HUBIN
CHAIRPERSONS: Mary Ann Grochowski
Beverly De Weese, Gary Niebuhr,
and THE CLOAK & CLUE SOCIETY

SET IN THE EXOTIC MID-WEST

THE 12TH ANNUAL ANTHONY BOUCHER MEMORIAL MYSTERY & DETECTION LITERATURE
WRITERS AND FAN CONVENTION

BOUCHERCON XII will take place October 9 - 11, 1981, at THE MARC PLAZA
HOTEL, 509 W. Wisconsin Ave., Milw., WI, 53203, Phone (414) 271-7250.

REGISTRATION FEE is a mere $15.00 for a weekend of mystery and mayhem
at THE BEER CITY CAPERS. Follow in the footsteps of notorious
authors and sinister plotters as you prowl the streets of Milwaukee,
the city of Gemütlichkeit!

GUEST OF HONOR: MS. HELEN McCLOY DRESSER.
Creator of the series starring the psychiatrist-detective,
Dr. Basil Willing, Ms. McCloy Dresser, has been an active
professional writer since 1918 when, at the age of 14, she sold
her first article. Since then, she has had an extremely versatile,
unique, and varied career, ranging from news correspondent to
art critic. In 1946, she married David Dresser, alias Brett Halliday
creator of Mike Shayne, and founded Torquil Publishing Co. She
was the first female president of The Mystery Writers of America.
She is still very active with her latest Dr. Willing Novel, Burn This
winning the 1980 Nero Wolfe award. Recently, the movie rights
to one of her most haunting novels, Through A Glass Darkly, was
sold to Bette Midler. The author of 29 novels, Ms. McCloy Dresser
was also the recipient of the Edgar Allen Poe Award from The
Mystery Writers of America for literary criticism of the mystery nove

OTHER SPEAKERS OF NOTE include great short story writers such as:
Robert Eckels, Edward Hoch, John Lutz, and Bill Pronzini. Novelists
planning to attend include:John Ball, Joe L. Hensley, Gene De Weese,
Rosemary Gatenby, Stuart Kaminsky, and Francis M. Nevins. Critics
in attendance will be in the company of Otto Penzler, Chris Steinbrunn
and Jon Breen.

OTHER FEATURED ATTRACTIONS include a booksellers room, films, autographin
sessions, a Sherlockian play, and a magician-detective.

THE PROGRAM will be diversified to suit the tastes of many fans from the
hard-boiled to the collector. It all begins at 6:00 P.M., October 9,
1981. Don't keep us in suspense. Send in your registration now!

MAIL Your $15.00 registration fee to Boucercon XII, c/o Mary Ann
Grochowski, 2009 S. 93 Street, West Allis, WI, 53227.